T0308088

❧ לוח השוואה ❧

1) ...

2) ...

אָסוּר	אָסוּר	אָסוּר	אָסוּר	אָסוּר	אָסוּר	אָסוּר
מֻתָּר	מֻתָּר	מֻתָּר	מֻתָּר	מֻתָּר	מֻתָּר	מֻתָּר
מֻתָּר	מֻתָּר	מֻתָּר	מֻתָּר	מֻתָּר	מֻתָּר	מֻתָּר
מֻתָּר	מֻתָּר	מֻתָּר	מֻתָּר	אָסוּר	אָסוּר	אָסוּר
מֻתָּר	מֻתָּר	מֻתָּר	אָסוּר	מֻתָּר	מֻתָּר	אָסוּר
אָסוּר	מֻתָּר	מֻתָּר	מֻתָּר	מֻתָּר	מֻתָּר	אָסוּר

אני לדודי

I Am For My Beloved

A Guide to Enhanced Intimacy for Married Couples

אני לדודי

I Am For My Beloved

A Guide to Enhanced Intimacy
for Married Couples

DAVID S. RIBNER AND TALLI Y. ROSENBAUM

URIM PUBLICATIONS
Jerusalem · New York

I Am For My Beloved
A Guide to Enhanced Intimacy for Married Couples
David Ribner and Talli Rosenbaum

Typeset by Studio Valdman

Printed in Israel

First Edition

ISBN 978-965-524-344-4

Urim Publications
P.O. Box 52287,
Jerusalem 9152102 Israel
www.UrimPublications.com

Library of Congress Cataloging-in-Publication Data

Names: Ribner, David S., 1946- author. | Rosenbaum, Talli Y., author.
Title: I am for my beloved : a guide to enhanced intimacy for married couples
/ David S. Ribner, Talli Y. Rosenbaum.
Description: First edition. | New York : Urim Publications, 2019. | Includes
bibliographical references.
Identifiers: LCCN 2019036005 | ISBN 9789655243444 (hardcover)
Subjects: LCSH: Intimacy (Psychology) | Man-woman relationships. | Married
people--Psychology. | Marriage--Religious aspects--Judaism.
Classification: LCC BF575.I5 R53 2019 | DDC 158.2--dc23
LC record available at https://lccn.loc.gov/2019036005

How to Make Love: Rabbinic Guidelines

From *Iggeret Hakodesh* ("Epistle on Holiness") by Nachmanides*
(Spain, 1194–1270), chapter six "On the Quality of Coitus" (ed. Chavel,
Jerusalem, 1964, pp. 335–6). Translated by Rabbi Dr. Zvi A. Yehuda

*Therefore, first introduce her into the mood with gentle words that
excite her emotion, appease her mind and delight her with joy. This
unites your mind and intention with hers. Say to her the words which
arouse in her passion, closeness, love, will, and erotic desire, and in part
evoke in her reverence for God, piety and modesty.*

*Never impose yourself upon her nor force her. For any sexual union
without an abundance of passion, love, and will is without the Divine
Presence. Do not quarrel with her nor act violently whenever coitus is
involved. The Talmud says (Pesachim 49b): "A lion ravishes and then
eats and has no shame." Rather, court and attract her to you first with
gracious and seductive, as well as refined and gentle, words, so that both
your intentions be for the sake of God. Furthermore, never cohabit with
your wife while she is asleep, for then you are not one with your hearts. It is
proper that you first awaken her with words of endearment and passion.*

*Do not hurry in arousing passion. Prolong until she is ready and
in a passionate mood. Approach her lovingly and passionately, so that
she reaches her orgasm first.*

---

* This work is a letter to a friend on the sanctity of matrimony and the art of love,
from a rabbinic-kabbalistic outlook. Since the 14th century the work has been
highly esteemed by moralists, mystics and Halachists alike, and frequently published and quoted. Since Scholem's article (in *Kiryat Sefer* XXI, 1944, 179 ff.) the
authorship is considered uncertain. Chavel in his preface (315ff.) believes the
author to be one of Nachmanides' contemporaries.

CONTENTS

Acknowledgments

We would like to thank the following colleagues who reviewed and provided helpful feedback on this manuscript. Thanks to Shifra Apter, Dr. Naomi Grumet, Rachel Hercman, Dr. Peggy Kleinplatz, Dr. Yehuda Krohn, Elisheva Liss, Dr. Mordechai Reich, Talya Roth, Sara Schapiro-Halberstam and Jordana Schoor. Your valuable comments, corrections and contributions are greatly appreciated.

Thank you to Tiferet Sigala for providing the graphics. Thank you to Shmuel Blitz, Mati Rosenbaum, and Sherry Zimmerman for your valuable publishing advice. Thank you to Sara Eisen and Raanan Rosenbaum for your creative input on the cover design.

Special thank you to the book's editor, Rabbi Alan Rosenbaum, who spent countless hours poring over the manuscript, fixing, correcting, and reminding us that when it comes to words, less is more.

Finally, we would like to thank our spouses and our children, whose encouragement, support and permission are deeply valued.

The quotations at the opening of each section are excerpts from "Jewish Marriage Ceremony and Matan Torah," by Rabbi Dr. Zvi A. Yehuda, of blessed memory, father of co-author Talli Rosenbaum. These remarks were delivered at her marriage to

Rabbi Alan Rosenbaum. Rabbi Yehuda was a prolific author, prominent educator and Talmudic scholar, who spent much of his formative years studying with one of the leading sages of his generation, Rabbi Avraham Yeshaya Karelitz (1878–1953), known as the *Chazon Ish*.

Rabbi Yehuda was also a romantic who, together with Talli's mother, Hassia, exemplified the ideals of passion, intimacy and commitment in their 56-year marriage.

I. INTRODUCTION

*There is a connection between Jewish marriage and Matan Torah –
the giving of the Torah at Sinai. The ceremony of Jewish marriage is
modeled after the experience of Matan Torah.*

*Torah is the living expression of the everlasting covenant – the love
bond – between God and Israel. In the prophetic words of God to His
people: "Ve'erastich Li Le'olam – I shall bind you to Me forever" (Ho-
sea 2:21). The celestial "betrothal" between God and people, Matan
Torah became the inspirational model for the traditional ceremony of
marriage between a Jewish man and a Jewish woman.*

T HIS BOOK IS intended for couples who wish to enrich their
marital and sexual lives and maintain passion and intimacy
throughout the life cycle, within the philosophy of traditional
Judaism.

We initially intended this book to be a guide to physical
intimacy for observant couples. We sought to help our readers
with basic information about sexual anatomy and physiology,

techniques, and positions, and to do so in a way that would be respectful of our culture of modesty.

As we proceeded, we chose to broaden the book's scope, acknowledging that a passionate marriage is not only about having good sex, but also about cultivating a mutually respectful and loving emotional relationship in accordance with Jewish values. We have provided ideas and suggestions that will enable you to have a more open and fulfilling intimate connection, both emotionally and physically, and we encourage you to discuss with one another the thoughts and feelings provoked by reading this book.

We are aware of our responsibilities to each reader, to our families and to the Jewish world in which we live. We recognize that not every concept discussed in this book may be consonant with your views, and we encourage consultation with your *halachic* authority about questions you may have.

We will provide a summary of the basics of sexuality, and how emotional and physical intimacy is interrelated. We will discuss how sexuality changes throughout the couple's life cycle, and we will provide suggestions on how to enhance emotional intimacy as well as physical pleasure.

Normative life cycle events such as childbirth and aging, as well as trauma or chronic illness, can have a negative effect on a couple's emotional and physical relationship, and we have provided tools for coping with stressful marital situations. We will also address the realities of living in accordance with the values of modesty, sexual exclusivity and sanctity in the modern world, and we will examine the subjects of pornography and infidelity, issues with which some couples may struggle.

In the interest of providing clear and useful information, this book provides a few illustrations and uses descriptive terminology. At the same time, we strive to use language that is respectful and professional. While newly married couples will find value in this book, it is not intended as a basic how-to guide for consummating marriage. For that we recommend Ribner and Rosenfeld's book, *Et Le'ehov: A Time to Love* (Gefen).

At the end of the book, we provide resources and additional reading suggestions.

CHAPTER 1
What is intimacy?

I NTIMACY IS A state of closeness between individuals. While often associated with romantic love, there are many types of intimacy – emotional, intellectual, spiritual, and of course, physical. Intimate relationships occur between friends, family members, work colleagues, as well as romantic partners.

In order to create intimacy with another, one must have a strong sense of self. This includes the development of a healthy self-image, and the ability to recognize and express one's feelings, sensations and ideas. Additionally, one must have developed a sense of others and how they relate and respond to you.

From initial parental attachment, the human developmental process includes becoming aware of one's self as well as learning the skills to interact with others. Interaction with siblings and friends provides children with the opportunity to experience and resolve conflict, name and express feelings, provide and accept empathy, and learn to trust. In adolescence, for example, when one shares a secret with a close friend, and he or she keeps that secret, one learns to share a confidence, thus creating the skills for intimacy.

Children learn skills of intimacy when they are taught to recognize, appreciate and love themselves and their bodies, when their emotions and sensations are validated by their parents, when their questions are answered honestly and when their boundaries are respected.

Creating real emotional as well as physical intimacy in a marriage requires the ability to know one's own feelings and sensations and to communicate them to one's partner. This requires several characteristics, including vulnerability, authenticity, bravery, curiosity and self-confidence, which we describe below. Someone who is extremely shy, for example, may struggle with the exposure of expressing his or her true feelings, which may be a barrier in building an intimate relationship.

Being authentic and genuine are basic to the creation of true intimacy. When beginning to date, young women and men may be advised or even instructed exactly what to say, what questions to ask, what to reveal, or what to hide. This behavior may inhibit the natural development of intimacy, which includes being genuine, curious about the other, exposing intimate details and secrets, and building trust.

In the development of real intimacy, a couple learns to communicate by staying curious, listening, validating each other's feelings, and providing empathy. While every relationship has its unique blend of various qualities, we would like to describe some of the basic aspects of an emotionally intimate relationship. Your connection with each other provides additional layers of pleasure and satisfaction when it takes place in a context of a strong emotional bond. The following are fundamental elements of creating this strong emotional bond:

Trust, vulnerability and acceptance – Your comfort in being open with each other depends to a great extent on the level of mutual trust, and the belief that your partner loves you as you are. For some couples, the hesitation to reveal fears and self-doubt may be a greater challenge than disrobing in each other's presence. The feeling of being accepted by your partner without judgment and without the expectation of fundamental change, allows you to share those places where you may feel vulnerable and uncertain, trusting in each other to never use this material in a harmful manner.

Tenderness, caring and affection – Couples should seek to experience a bond that conveys feelings of love and connectedness. This is more likely to occur when these feelings are a pervasive aspect of your lives. The words "tenderness," "caring," and "affection" represent a wide range of positive emotions that ideally convey the way you feel and communicate with each other regularly. Styles of communication may vary. Some of you may be more verbal, and others more action-oriented. However you do it, such messages will surely strengthen your intimate bonds.

Open communication – You do not have to tell your partner that he or she seems to have put on a few extra pounds, or share every private thought and feeling. However, we do encourage a level of communication that is clear and unambiguous, and that is intended to convey messages in as positive and assertive a manner as possible. Trust and affection certainly play a role, allowing for disagreement without feelings of rejection or devaluing. Bear in mind, though, that no one is telepathic, so do not assume you know each other's thoughts or feelings. That's what words are for. Rather than refer to what your partner did, which can elicit a defensive reaction, stick to "I feel" statements that convey your experience, and ask if your partner can mirror you back to make sure he or she really understands you.

Curiosity – An essential component of developing relationships with others, whether in a social, academic, or occupational setting, is the desire to know more about them. Curiosity is what helped form your relationship with your spouse as well. Curiosity helps couples stay attuned to one another and to one another's experiences, thoughts and feelings. Staying curious about our partner's reactions and behaviors, rather than becoming reactive or making assumptions, helps to avoid and resolve conflicts.

Expressions of acknowledgment and gratitude – No one enjoys feeling taken for granted. Simple expressions of appreciation and thankfulness for both the expected and unexpected gestures can create a positive atmosphere and provide each partner with the feeling that they are being seen and valued.

Acts of kindness – Successful couples do more for each other than just the minimum necessary to maintain home and family. These couples, by action more than word, seek to make each other's lives that much happier, and they do so often. Even more significant is that they do so out of regard for their partners and not because they expect something in return. Each of these acts conveys a message of investing in your emotional intimacy.

Mechanisms for healing and repair – Every couple will confront circumstances when things do not work out, when communication fails, and when expectations are unmet. Moving beyond these moments requires the development of mechanisms to repair emotional damage and to heal from the hurt caused by these issues. Of particular importance is that neither of you become a "grievance collector," raising a host of past issues whenever you confront the next conflict. The more efficient these mechanisms of closure, the less risk you will have of accumulating emotional scar tissue.

Independent growth and development – As you move along in your lives, you should take great satisfaction in watching each other continue to grow and develop. Each of you may have different career paths, interests and places to invest your time and energy. The more each of you finds satisfaction in your own lives, the more you will feel confident in supporting your partner's advancement. This will not diminish all that you share with each other; it will enhance your relationship and enrich the emotional and intellectual quality of your lives. Your bonds will be that much stronger.

Self-awareness – Stay attuned to yourself. Know when you are feeling triggered or defensive, or when you are beginning to feel angry. Being able to express yourself calmly is better than ignoring your feelings and allowing resentment to build, which may lead to aggressive or passive-aggressive reactions later.

Novelty – We recommend that couples do not take each other for granted. Going out on a "blind date," role-playing, and experiencing new and different places and situations together will help retain a romantic atmosphere and keep the relationship alive.

CHAPTER 2
Intimacy skills

T HE FOLLOWING SKILLS are essential in the creation and maintenance of real and lasting intimacy in your marriage.

- Really *listen* to your partner. Studies show that feeling listened to, understood and cared about improves relationship satisfaction.

- Empathizing is usually better than trying to fix. Sometimes your partner just wants to vent. You may not be able to fix what's wrong, but saying something like "Wow, that sounds really hard" lets them know that you "get it." Ask your partner how they prefer you to react when they have a problem that they want to discuss. Most people want their partners to just listen and empathize.

- You aren't always responsible for your partner's mood. If your partner is upset, don't assume it is because of you, and don't become defensive. Remember that it is his or her mood, not yours.

- Sex is not an entitlement, a reward, nor a punishment. Sex should be mutual, consensual, pleasurable and private. It will take time to learn what you and your partner like. Don't set goals and expectations, or make it feel like work.

- Fight right and make up. All couples will have

disagreements and arguments. It is important to know how to fight, and how to recover. If you are feeling defensive, say so, and if you feel too angry or reactive, request a timeout. Make sure you initiate a follow-up discussion when you are calmer, and use "I feel" statements rather than blaming, shaming, or criticizing. Allow yourself to be vulnerable enough to say, "I think I may have upset you" or "Let's resolve this. I don't want to fight anymore."

- Be affectionate – not only when sex is on the agenda. There are many ways to value touch. Cuddling, hugging, stroking and massaging add to your feelings of bonding and attachment. (See Chapters 8, 9 and 14 for more specifics.)

- Continue to date. Just because you are married doesn't mean you should stop doing fun things together. Make sure to create space for quality time and recreational activities. Once children and grandchildren start coming, continue to value and invest in your time with each other.

- Be there for each other, be one another's friend, lover and confidant.

These skills will provide the context that will strengthen the development of your physical intimacy.

In the following chapters, we will provide guidelines for enhancing mutual sexual satisfaction. May you experience passion, intimacy, love, compassion, trust and commitment in your journey together.

II. SEXUAL RELATIONS: VALUES AND ATTITUDES

The Chuppah – the wedding canopy – dramatizes the dimension of intimacy and privacy. Paradoxically, however, it is positioned under the open sky, which dramatizes the dimension of publicness and openness. Jewish marriage is, on the one hand the most private institution between two private individuals, and on the other hand, the most public institution, of concern to the entire Jewish community. So is the Torah, both private and public; its experience both personal and communal.

CHAPTER 3
The challenge of "succeeding"

B EFORE ADDRESSING THE subject of sexual relations, it is important to acknowledge the influence of Jewish law on marital and sexual life. The laws of Jewish family purity (from here on referred to as *taharat hamishpachah*) require that married couples abstain from physical and sexual contact for the duration of the length of the woman's menstrual period, plus an additional seven days. This is known as the *niddah* period. At the end of this separation, a woman immerses in the ritual bath (*mikveh*). Afterwards, the couple may resume physical and sexual contact. This system's influence extends beyond the domain of marital sexual life. Orthodox couples are expected, prior to marriage, to refrain from physical contact. Yet, there is an expectation that intercourse takes place shortly after the wedding. For many couples, the focus on "succeeding" at intercourse disrupts their ability to relax together and slowly experience touch and pleasure. The first days, weeks, and often months, may include feelings of anxiety, pressure and distress.

Some couples have intercourse on their wedding night, but the memories of that first time may be negative, as it may have felt awkward, forced, painful, or too quick. According to *halachah* (Jewish law) couples married for the first time must physically separate and enter a *niddah* period after the initial act of intercourse. Some couples may be unsure if penetration has occurred, and may seek counsel of rabbis or premarital counselors. This can sabotage the couple's sense of privacy, autonomy and comfort.

For some young Orthodox couples who are accustomed to being successful, whether as youth group leaders, students or professionals, perceiving themselves as "failing" at what has become a mission to "accomplish" is dissonant with their role identities and is accompanied by feelings of shame and frustration, emotions they may continue to experience throughout the marriage. The initial difficulty with consummating the marriage is usually a cause of distress and anxiety, and the common language used is "we tried," "we failed" or "we succeeded." This language is often perpetuated with other supposed "milestones" of sexual engagement, including the "achievement" of orgasm, simultaneous orgasm, or orgasm during intercourse. Additionally, these couples may assume that everyone else's sex life is ideal.

Sex should not feel like work, and the only goals should be that both partners are willing and open to pleasure and connection. The following story illustrates this idea:

> You embark on a three-hour hike. The tour guide says, "At the end of the trail there is a beautiful view."
>
> You begin the trail thinking, "When will I get there?" and spend most of the three hours focused on what it is you will see when you arrive.
>
> As you are about to reach your destination, a fellow hiker joins you. You ask him if he too, is looking forward to seeing the view at the end of the journey.

The fellow hiker turns to you with enthusiasm and says. "Sure, but did you see the amazing trees and blossoms we passed? Did you taste the figs from the tree, and see the gorgeous brooks and streams? Even if I didn't make it to the end, I would be satisfied with all the beauty I experienced today."

At that moment, you realize that you were so fixated on reaching the goal that you completely missed out on enjoying the journey.

For too many couples, sex is goal-oriented. At the very beginning, rather than focusing on pleasure and connection, young couples are unfortunately encouraged to "succeed" at having sex, and this message may have far-reaching negative echoes. Physical intimacy is much more than sexual intercourse, and we will assist you to enjoy the many steps of this journey.

CHAPTER 4
The challenge of *taharat hamishpachah*

T HE OBSERVANCE OF *taharat hamishpachah* is a central aspect of our lives that affects sexuality. The cycle of complete abstention during *niddah* periods, culminating with sexual engagement and intercourse upon *mikveh* immersion can be experienced as an exciting, recurrent cycle of longing and renewal. For many couples, though, this rhythm is challenging, engendering pressure and obligation, and retriggering the initial feelings of sexual intercourse as a goal and a requirement. The drive to get together because time is running out, or the difficult times that ensue when you want to hug but cannot, are part of the realities of this system.

Lack of spontaneity, having sex by the calendar, pressure to have sex before the permissible time expires and desire for physical affection when it is forbidden are challenges that couples in our practices have cited. Furthermore, some couples may have differing views regarding how to observe these laws. We encourage couples to communicate openly and honestly about these issues. Mutual respect, compromise and creativity are necessary to resolve these conflicts and most couples can achieve a comfortable rhythm for this aspect of their lives.

Ten Tips for Mikveh Night

The Eden Center is a Jerusalem-based initiative dedicated to enhancing the mikveh experience and connecting it to women's health and intimacy education. Dr. Naomi Grumet, its founder, offers the following ten tips:

The results of my research indicate that there is a range of reactions that both men and women have to "*mikveh* night." Some love the excitement that the abstinence brings, and feel that it puts their desires in sync. Others find it very stressful and feel pressure to perform. At different points in life, couples can vacillate along the continuum between these two extremes. Though not irreversible, *mikveh* night can set the tone for what will happen during the rest of the month. If you or your partner find *mikveh* night to be a source of pressure, if you don't enjoy the *mikveh* experience, or if you resent how *mikveh* determines your sexual schedule, you are not alone. For some people, these feelings are eased when they agree to remove all sexual expectations from the evening. The couples that get the most out of *mikveh* night seem to be those who use the time leading up to that evening to connect and to communicate about their desires and expectations. Following are some *mikveh* night tips that can be beneficial even for those who do not choose to engage in intercourse on *mikveh* night:

1. *Mikveh* night isn't automatically magical. Clarifying expectations and communicating your needs and desires can be beneficial.

2. Set aside the time to be with each other. Even if it means cancelling other obligations, allocating this time as consecrated lets your partner know that you are investing in both the emotional and physical aspects of your relationship.

3. Start in advance. Send notes, SMS's or put a chocolate on his/her pillow to let your spouse know you are looking forward. These can help set the tone and enhance desire.

4. Intimacy, rather than "sex," should be the goal for the night. Remember that 0 to 100 is a lot for many people; sexual intimacy consists of much beyond intercourse.

5. Set the stage. Small gestures can make a big difference. Husband, while your wife is at the *Mikveh*, think about what household tasks she would appreciate you having accomplished in the house. Wives, before going to the *Mikveh*, attempt to finish your family and professional obligations so that you are both mentally and physically available and ready to be together.

6. Have fun –do something you enjoy doing together. The desire to be together physically comes naturally when partners connect in other ways.

7. Use this time to explore. It can be as simple as a massage, lingerie, a romantic dinner or a head-to-toe caress.

8. If children or prior engagements get in the way, make an alternate plan like waking up early the next morning or setting aside another night.

9. Add a twist. Switch off who will be in charge of the evening, and surprise each other with fun/romantic/ intimate things that make it exciting to get back together, and put you both in the mood.

10. Many couples are comfortable with simply reconnecting. Others look to *Mikveh* night as a time to spice things up. Either way is fine! For those looking to spice things up, this can be a time to introduce new ways to enhance your sex life. (See Section V, 'Sexual Enhancement'.)

CHAPTER 5
A mindful approach to experiencing intimacy

A s couples move through the life cycle, goal orientation surrounding sex may focus primarily on success in achieving orgasm, becoming pregnant, or setting a minimal weekly frequency. Pressure to engage in relations, or different expectations regarding frequency may contribute to the feeling of sex as a chore to check off the to-do list, and may engender guilt in the partner who isn't feeling "enough" desire. Sex should be a place to connect and experience pleasure rather than something to accomplish.

We experience sex in a multi-dimensional way. Thoughts about sex are influenced by the attitudes, values and cultural influences with which we were raised. Our feelings and sensations around sex may be influenced by what is occurring in the relationship, including power struggles and the ways partners trigger one another. Of course, physical factors, such as hormones and exhaustion, can affect how we experience pleasure.

Approaching intimacy with mindfulness is a concept that can enhance marital intimacy on all levels – physical, emotional, and cognitive. Mindful sex involves reducing thoughts, and in particular, judgments and expectations ("Am I good enough, do I look OK, what if I or my partner doesn't reach orgasm?"). Mindfulness encourages being in the moment and focusing on every aspect of the journey, rather than focusing on an end goal. To illustrate this concept, think about the simple activity of taking a shower. To some, it may be a basic activity undertaken for daily hygiene. It can be done while thinking about the list of chores that need to be accomplished for that day. A mindful shower, however, can involve reveling in the sensory experience of being embraced by warm water while enjoying the sweet aroma of lavender.

"Beginner's mind" is a mindfulness-based concept that encourages individuals to approach a familiar experience as if they are experiencing it for the very first time. "Beginner's mind" eliminates the expectation that it will be "as good or better" than the time before, but will rather be its own unique experience. This lowers both expectations and disappointments. Cuddling, for example, can be experienced mindfully as a uniquely pleasurable and satisfying intimate activity, even if it doesn't lead to intercourse.

Mindfulness encourages full presence and acceptance of thoughts, feelings and sensations, and discourages self-judgment and constant striving for success. For the many religious and ultra-Orthodox Jews we see in our practices, approaching intimate relations with mindfulness may seem challenging. We are a purposeful and goal-oriented people and our behavior is informed by a strong moral conscience. Some clients recoil at the idea of "wasting time" luxuriating in the shower, when we are conditioned that "the day is short, the work to be performed is much, and the Master is insistent" (*Avot* 2:15). In addition, the laws of ritual purity that restrict physical contact during the *niddah* period and promote full sexual engagement after *mikveh* immersion, may make sex feel like something that is either "off" or "on," rather than at times "on a low flame."

We suggest that Jewish tradition, at its essence, does promote mindfulness. Do we not value the enhancement of rituals such as the *havdalah* service, by deeply inhaling the aroma of the spices and acknowledging the burning flame? Do we not choose the most flawless *Etrog* that pleases the eye? We do this to enhance the observance of the *mitzvah*. We also attempt to pray with full intent, rather than let our minds drift off as we utter the words. Praying with intent, *kavana,* is about being mindful.

Mindfulness practitioners promote setting aside one day a week which is screen-free, where all communication devices are turned off so that one may meditate, focus on one's loved ones and spend time with one's family. Sound familiar? That piece of information usually sells clients on the value of mindfulness.

Mindful intimacy involves setting aside time for intentional, planned dates, communicating what you would like, finding out what your partner wants, and acknowledging and showing love and appreciation for one another, both inside and outside the bedroom.

Sex is not something you "have," but rather an expression of an intimate and erotic energy that a couple mutually shares. It may be expressed in the bedroom, but it does not begin there. It is present in the way the couple engages, and even looks at one another. According to the "good enough sex model" introduced by sex therapists and authors Michael Metz and Barry McCarthy, sex can be valued for its many meanings. Sometimes it is a place of intimacy, bonding and being united. Other times it may be a "quickie" for relieving stress. Sex can be experienced with playfulness and laughter, and sometimes with seriousness and even spirituality. It does not need to be the same each time or even the same for both partners.

While two people are making love with one another, they may be experiencing it differently – one may enjoy physical closeness while the other seeks an intensely sexual experience.

Furthermore, "good enough sex" doesn't demand goals or expectations of erections, orgasms or intercourse, but rather appreciates the value of experiencing the journey of intimacy with minimal judgment and maximal presence of mind. And of course, love.

CHAPTER 6
Sex and sanctity

O NE OF US treated a young couple that complained of a vague unease and dissatisfaction with their sex life. Their overall marital relationship was honest, respectful and supportive; both expressed sexual desire, and there were no functional problems, traumatic histories or inhibitions. Finally, they were asked to describe their bedroom. When they got to the part about pictures of famous rabbis on the walls, the therapist had a reasonably good sense as to the nature of their problem and a simple way to solve it.

Many religious couples seek to live lives in which sanctity is a goal, and pictures of rabbis in the home symbolize this. Some couples may, however, struggle with how to keep the bedroom "holy," as well. We suggest that creating a sacred space that includes only the two of you in an intimate setting is in itself the meaning of sexual sanctity. That is the place and time to think and focus on each other. Pictures of religious figures can distract from what should be the only focus in that hallowed bedroom space.

We believe that the bedroom should not feel disconnected from religious values. A well-known Talmudic story (*Berachot* 62a) relates how the sage, Rav Kahana, hid under the bed of the great scholar, Rav, while the latter was engaged in intimate behavior with his wife. Rav Kahana was discovered by Rav, who ordered him to leave. Rav Kahana, who was surprised to hear Rav engaging playfully with his wife as though they were newlyweds, responded, "but it is Torah, and I must learn."

The very manner in which we behave, learn, work, eat, pray, and, even make love, affirms our values and beliefs.

The core values and behavioral expectations that guide our day-to-day interactions have equal application in the bedroom. Making space for others in our lives, respecting boundaries, sensitivity, supporting each other's individuality and seeking to develop together are all qualities which enhance a couple's sex life just as much as they enhance our communal and familial fabric.

A couple's sexual vocabulary should reflect the uniqueness of their relationship. The words and expressions that work for one couple may not be practical for others; as long as communication is clear and neither spouse takes offense, these private codes should be functional and hopefully arousing and connecting.

Couples should develop a sufficiently effective level of self-awareness to determine if their hesitancy about any sexual option is truly rooted in *halachic* doubts. Regrettably, *halachic* questions can be a handy tool with which to avoid confronting personal or relational issues. Conversely, *halachic* acceptability should not be the only determinant in deciding about sexual activities, nor should a rabbi's determined allowance of an activity entitle one partner to demand it from the other. Of equal importance to the *halachic* concern, is to determine each partner's desire, willingness, comfort and/or hesitations regarding the particular activity.

A successful sex life requires a sense of freedom from the well-meaning advice of others. Trust your instincts and be sensitive to one another, without being too concerned about the shared experiences of friends, relatives and educators. It is the absence of this sense of freedom that contributes to many sexual dysfunctions.

As an observant Jew, one can be religious and be sexual without disconnecting from either. So, feel good and guilt-free about the intimacy you share with your partner, and about taking the time to enhance this aspect of your marriage.

CHAPTER 7
Consulting with clergy

I N OUR EXPERIENCE as sex therapists, some of our clients, both couples and individuals, express concern as to whether various aspects of sexual thoughts, behaviors, or fantasies fall within acceptable *halachic* boundaries. Our general response is that such questions related to Jewish law should be directed to a *halachic* authority competent in matters of human sexuality. However, before speaking with clergy about these issues, we offer some guidelines to help you get the most from your consultation.

- Sexuality is an area of particular expertise within Jewish law, and not every teacher or rabbi is sufficiently learned or experienced to be helpful. Ask your religious advisor about their expertise in this realm.

- Each couple's intimate life will have aspects unique to them. Consult an authority who knows you personally, who will take the time to explore the issues and who will offer guidelines appropriate to your current circumstances.

- Both of you should be part of this process, as the rabbi needs to hear both of your perspectives and concerns. Find clergy who inspire confidence and who are comfortable speaking with both women and men.

- Rabbis and teachers are human, and have their own sex

lives and histories. While we wish for the highest level of objectivity and empathy, as with all aspects of life, these are by no means guaranteed. Make sure your expectations are realistic.

- Few Orthodox *halachic* authorities are trained as certified sex therapists. Moreover, the ethics of a professional therapist providing *halachic* guidelines is questionable, as therapists are expected to refrain from presenting a judgmental stance or religious agenda.

- Discuss and try to reach agreement about what you wish to ask before you leave the house. Even if you have separate concerns or approaches, don't ambush each other in the rabbi's study.

- Be as clear and precise as you are able, with yourselves and with the rabbi. Find language with which you are comfortable, and be prepared to explain, to help ensure that you are understood. If you are genuinely confused and intend to request rabbinic direction, then you are likely in the right place. If, however, you know in advance that you will find the rabbi's response to be unacceptable, don't raise the question. In such a situation, you are not asking for rabbinic guidance, but are merely seeking approbation for your existing perspectives.

- Unless your rabbi is trained as a marital therapist, do not make use of the rabbi's services to determine if you and your partner are compatible. If compatibility is your concern or if your agenda is to justify leaving the relationship, visit a certified marital and/or sex therapist.

- If any question you are asked seems overly intrusive, do not feel any obligation to answer. You are in control of the information you wish to impart. Trust your intuition if you are feeling uncomfortable about revealing too much to a rabbi. If you are in doubt about your contact with a rabbi, speak with someone knowledgeable in these areas.

- Most importantly, if any aspect of your contact with a *halachic* authority feels "off," trust your instincts and find someone else.

- In many modern Orthodox communities, female religious advisors and female authority figures have undergone extensive training in both *halachah* and human sexuality. Several options exist for couples, and particularly for women, who prefer to consult with women. For example, *Yoatzot Halachah*, trained in answering questions related to *taharat hamishpachah*, receive advanced training in women's sexual health.

III: UNDERSTANDING SEXUALITY

*As Torah is both a unifying force, molding and cementing a commu-
nity, a people, and at the same time upholding the ultimate significance
of each and every individual, so too is Jewish marriage.*

S EXUALITY DETERMINES AND perpetuates the continuity
of life and is an energy that motivates, compels and drives
behaviors. On a personal level, it is part of the self, and through
that self, one can feel alive, express love, and create a family.

Emotional and physical intimacy and sexual relations are a
valued part of a couple's relationship, providing the opportunity to
experience closeness, joy, pleasure, satisfaction, security, bonding,
playfulness and even a spiritual connection.

Sex can be an expression of passion, creativity, and love. It
involves holding on to yourself while letting go, feeling secure

while taking risks, and being in the moment with all your senses while trusting, accepting and sharing.

Setting up a goal of so-called "great sex" with each interaction can be confusing, frustrating and inhibiting. A much more realistic expectation is that sexual relations should almost always be pleasurable, and perhaps enhanced by '"fireworks" from time to time. Sex should not be painful, neither physically nor emotionally, and if it is, see a sexual health professional. Don't be swayed by the media, statistics or a chat with your sister-in-law. The only measure of your enjoyment is your own. An additional factor is that your sexual interests and abilities will likely change throughout the course of your lifetime – ask any first-time parent! We will describe these changes in greater detail later in this book.

Finally, it is important to be able to experience the sexual relationship as an expression of an intimate and erotic energy that a couple shares. This erotic energy may be expressed in many ways. Sometimes it is experienced with playfulness and laughter, sometimes with nurturing and comforting hugs, and sometimes with verbal expressions of deep love and commitment. The expectation that these erotic expressions only occur when sexual intercourse takes place is likely to inhibit intimate communication. When you can engage together without pressure to perform, when you can learn that sex is a place to be rather than something to do, you can learn to appreciate the value of experiencing the journey of intimacy with minimal judgment and maximal presence of mind.

So, is there great sex? Yes, there can be, and we will offer some tips about enhancing your sex life later in the book. In addition, we will also provide a list of reliable resources should you wish to do some exploring together.

Chapter 8
Sexual communication

O PEN COMMUNICATION IS one of the primary elements in maintaining a mutually satisfying and secure feeling of physical intimacy. There are many sources of information regarding the basic tools and skills of successful marital communication, such as empathy and active listening (see the references at the end of this book). Rather than repeat them here, we offer some concrete guidelines for comfortably discussing sex with each other. We hope you will experience some immediate improvement, but if you are like most couples, expect to need practice, and be helped along by patience, good will and a sense of humor.

- As compatible as you both may be, each of you came to your marriage with years of different experiences, family and communal norms and values, and life expectations. Consequently, you probably look at your sex lives differently from one another. Comfortably discussing these differences will avoid considerable stress and help you steer clear of making unwarranted and potentially damaging assumptions about each other. Since you can't read each other's minds, do not expect your partner to understand you unless you can be clearly expressive.

- Develop a sexual vocabulary that works for both of you, specifically names of body parts (e.g., finding alternate terms for penis or vagina if you want), as well as intimate activities ("sexual intercourse" may sound too technical). This language is exclusively yours. It must flow for both of you, and it must be open to change as you move through your lives. Also, make sure you clearly define the terms to avoid misunderstanding. The request to "be together" may mean engaging in intercourse for one spouse, while to the other, it may mean spending time together sitting on the couch.

- Establish a policy that each of you can suggest any sexual activity, and by the same token each of you can safely say no. This kind of intimate exchange requires a high level of trust – ensuring that these requests and responses are not meant to demean or cause distress. Achieving this level of comfort may take some trial and error, but it's worth the effort.

- Turning down a sexual suggestion should be done with thoughtfulness. Causing your partner to feel rejected does little to enhance an intimate atmosphere. Try offering a modification of the invitation or suggesting an alternate sexual activity known to be pleasing to both of you. If the timing is off, make a date for another opportunity. (Saying "some other time" is often not enough, and could be interpreted as rejection.) And of course, expressing caring and concern – saying "I love you" – always goes a long way to enhancing your emotional intimacy.

- Perhaps more important than talking with each other about sexual activities is sharing your feelings. We each bring multiple emotions into our marital relationship and they can range from warmth and eager anticipation to anxiety and self-doubt. Revealing these emotions reflects the trust you have in one another and can significantly contribute to your sense of closeness.

- There may be a number of potential challenges to sharing your feelings, particularly when your emotions are difficult to identify let alone describe. Many people find that their vocabulary of emotions may be somewhat limited, lacking the precision to truly express how they are feeling. The ability to effectively express your own emotions as well as listen to and contain your partner's emotions requires patience, and may take time to learn.

- Openness with each other should enable you to overcome these challenges, but if you get stuck in your attempts to effectively communicate feelings, see a trained marital counselor.

- Not everyone is comfortable with verbal communication although practice can bring improvement. For some, nonverbal cues are preferable. Because most of us tend to be less experienced in this area, and since nonverbal cues can be easily misconstrued, couples should invest in understanding and clarifying each other's nonverbal messages before attributing meaning to them.

CHAPTER 9
Intimate touch

A MONG THE TROUBLESOME sexual messages conveyed by current media is the emphasis on sexual intercourse and orgasm as the ultimate goals of physical intimacy. In addition to raising often unrealistic performance challenges, these expectations severely limit consideration of additional intimate options which couples may find mutually enjoyable.

We wish to offer an alternative message.

Every inch of your skin contains myriad nerve cells, which means that everywhere on your body you have the potential for enjoyable intimate contact. In fact, touch is the first sense a newborn uses to be connected with its world, and it is the only sense that does not diminish with age.

Exploring each other from head to toe can provide you with new opportunities for touching and being touched, and for discovering how to please each other in ways you did not know before. Whether caressing, massaging or just simply exploring, learning to appreciate each other's skin can significantly expand your intimate options.

Location, as well, can offer further sensual opportunities. Sitting on your sofa and gently appreciating each other's faces with your fingertips can be as intimate and instructive as slowly bathing each other in a warm shower. Feel free to use your imaginations, but equally, feel free to let your partner know the limits of your comfort zone.

Here are a few additional tips for getting more pleasure from your skin:

- Body lotions or oils, scented or unscented, can add a new dimension to your intimate touch. Start with a few drops and then be guided by your partner's response. Check the label to make sure whatever you are using can be safely applied to sensitive areas.

- The issue of trimming or removing body hair, especially pubic hair, has engendered considerable discussion. The practice has a long cultural history (see *Sanhedrin* 21a) and has provoked diverse and sometimes intense responses. If one of you is requesting this of your partner, you will need to honestly discuss motivation, expectations, physical and emotional consequences and any related health issues. Ultimately any decision must be based on the full control each of you has over your own body.

- Naked, full-body contact can be sensual without being sexual. Either standing or lying in bed together, you can allow yourselves to caress and be caressed, at times with gentle genital touch and at times without. This experience can be intimately reassuring, without any performance expectations. And of course, if you both so desire, you can take it further.

IV. UNDERSTANDING
HOW SEX WORKS

Ish (man) and Isha (woman) together create a unity, a oneness. None-theless, each retains his or her individuality. The ideal in the creation of humankind is two creations – a man and a woman, each maintaining the integrity of individuality, even in their loving unity.

NORMATIVE HETEROSEXUAL FUNCTIONING implies that there is motivation and desire to engage in sex, an experience of pleasurable arousal and possible orgasm, and the ability to comfortably engage in and enjoy sexual activities, including intercourse. Sexual satisfaction is generally defined by the existence of most of these elements, most of the time. Sexual dysfunction describes repeated difficulty in one or more of these areas of sexual functioning.

The following section will provide some basic information on the biology of sex.

CHAPTER 10
Female and male sexual anatomy and physiology

Female anatomy and physiology

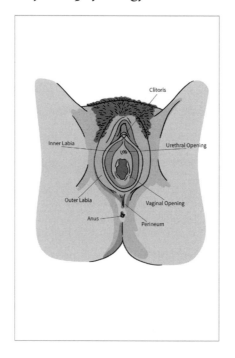

External view

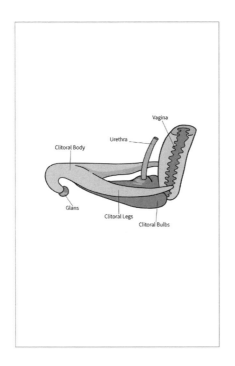

Internal view

The *vulva* is the entire visible genital area, from the area of the pubic hair down to the anus. Visible externally are the *perineum, labia, urethra,* and *clitoris* and the *vaginal opening.*

The *perineum* is the area that connects the anus to the vagina. It is a hairless area of skin, which sometimes tears, or is intentionally cut, during childbirth, in a procedure known as an episiotomy.

The *labia* are the flaps of tissue that fold together over the vagina. The *outer labia* are generally covered with hair, and the *inner labia* are smooth and rich in blood supply. The *labia* have sensory nerve endings that are sensitive to touch and are a source of sexual stimulation.

Inside the folds of the labia, above the entrance to the vagina, lies the *urethra,* a small opening for the passage of urine. Above that is the *glans* of the *clitoris,* the most sensitive area of a woman's genitals. The *clitoral glans* is normally obstructed by a hood that retracts and is exposed during sexual stimulation. The function of the *clitoris* is to provide sexual pleasure, and when stimulated, it enlarges and becomes erect due to increased blood flow in that area. While the *glans* is visible to the eye, most of the *clitoris* lies internally. It is composed of two legs, known as *crura,* which surround the vagina and *clitoral body.* The main cylindrical region of the clitoris contains two columns of spongy erectile tissue that fill with blood causing it to enlarge during sexual arousal.

Just inside the inner lips is the opening to the vagina. Prior to the first episode of sexual intercourse, the vagina is often, but not always, partially surrounded by a thin membranous layer known as the *hymen.* There are many misconceptions related to the presence of the hymen as proof of a woman's virginity. In fact, there are sexually active women who retain hymenal tissue. If an intact hymen is penetrated in an aggressive fashion, there can be large amounts of bleeding. If, however, the woman is aroused, lubricated, and relaxed, penetration can occur with minimal trauma to the hymen, and often little or no bleeding. The *vagina* is tube-shaped and about six inches in length. At the tip of the vagina is the *cervix,* which opens to the *uterus.* Women who have not been sexually active and have not used tampons, may not be familiar with this area and may have difficulty locating their vaginal opening. The first time many young religious women become aware of this area is upon receiving instruction to examine themselves with a cloth, as part of the ritual required in preparation for the *mikveh.* It is important to note that, while the vagina may appear narrow, it has the capacity to expand (as during childbirth) and contract, and can comfortably allow the entrance of just about any sized penis. Lying directly inside the opening to the vagina are muscles known as the *pelvic floor muscles.* Learning how to contract and then relax these muscles, helps women with awareness of their genital area, and facilitates autonomy and control with initial penetration experiences, such as inserting a tampon or self-examination, as well as with intercourse.

Male anatomy and physiology

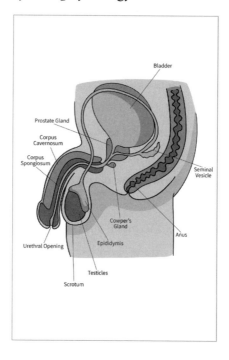

The male genitalia are composed of the penis, generally the most sensitive area, and the *scrotum*, which is the pouch below. The *scrotum* houses the *testicles* where sperm is produced. Mature sperm cells travel from there to the *epididymis*, which lie on top of the testicles. The head or *glans* of the penis houses the *urethra*, the opening where urine and semen pass. There are tubes of spongy tissue inside the penis known as *corpus cavernosa* and *corpus spongiosum*. With sexual arousal, this tissue fills with blood and causes the penis to become erect. Penile erection is a sign of male sexual arousal. At this stage, some fluid may be released from the urethra before ejaculation. This fluid is produced in the *Cowper's gland,* which lies underneath the *prostate.* During ejaculation, rhythmic contractions cause the sperm to travel through the *prostate gland* and *seminal vesicles,* where secretions rich in nutrients combine with them to form *semen,* which is expelled through the *urethra opening.*

Chapter 11
Sexual functioning

THE WORKINGS OF sexual physiology can be likened to that of an automobile. A car runs on gas, but the brakes provide regulation. Our systems are designed with accelerators which facilitate sexual behavior, and inhibitors that limit, control, and nuance our sexual behavior.

Sexual physiology is governed by the autonomic nervous system, the part of the nervous system that regulates automatic processes such as heart rate, breathing and digestion. When one's senses are stimulated through touch or smell, sight, thoughts, or feelings of attraction, the autonomic nervous system sends signals to the brain triggering the process of sexual arousal. This system is excitatory as it stimulates the sexual response. We also have an inhibitory system to regulate that response. The inhibitory system, which is governed by our more cognitive, rational brain area, the frontal lobe, ensures that sexual behavior occurs with thinking and executive functioning. When arousal reaches a peak, orgasm occurs.

Sexual function is generally divided into four stages: *desire, arousal, orgasm* and *resolution*. The sequence of these stages may differ amongst individuals.

Desire is complex in humans, and has both biological as well as cognitive roots. Desire is governed by hormones, and can be affected by medical conditions or medications, but is also greatly influenced by contextual factors such as stress and relationship issues. At certain times in a couple's life cycle, such as during the postpartum period, or at various stages of aging, hormonal changes combined with fatigue and stress can contribute to decreased sexual desire. It is important to be aware that this is a natural phenomenon, and not necessarily an indication of marital difficulties.

Sexual *arousal* is a sensual feeling of excitement and pleasure, during which physiological changes occur that cause the body to be receptive to sex. In women, the various changes that occur during arousal include widening and hardening of the nipples, and increased blood flow to the labia, vagina, and clitoris. The vagina widens in preparation for intercourse. Cells in the vagina secrete fluid to moisten and lubricate the vaginal walls, facilitating easier penetration. This demonstrates the importance of feeling sexually aroused when engaging in intercourse. The natural process of arousal prevents pain and excessive friction. In males, the corpus spongiosum fills with blood, facilitating erection of the penis, which is the main physical indicator of sexual arousal in men.

Orgasm is considered the peak of sexual pleasure. During orgasm, there is an increase in heart rate and breathing. In women, rhythmic contractions of the vaginal and pelvic floor muscles occur. In males, rhythmic contractions take place as well, leading to ejaculation of semen.

It is important to be aware that most women require

stimulation of the clitoris in order to reach orgasm. While some women reach orgasm through intercourse itself, others require external stimulation of the clitoris, directly or indirectly, with manual touch, oral stimulation, or the use of an object such as a vibrator. Couples should feel free to explore ways to bring one another to orgasm without setting unrealistic goals, such as simultaneous orgasms. Some women can experience more than one orgasm during sex, however, having only one orgasm does not indicate that a problem exists. Men generally experience only one orgasm and require a period of time for a subsequent erection and orgasm.

Resolution is the final stage, when the body cools down and physiologically returns to normal. The heart rate and breathing decrease, and the swelling of organs resolves. It is a period of feeling calm, relaxed, satisfied and closer to each other.

CHAPTER 12
Female sexual desire

MASTERS AND JOHNSON, the pioneer sex researchers who studied and named the domains of sexual functioning in the 1950s, found differences between men and women's sexual arousal and response. Specifically, the period of arousal to orgasm is longer for women, while men can go very quickly from initial arousal to plateau to ejaculation. Furthermore, while men go from orgasm to resolution, some women can experience several orgasms in one sexual experience.

Masters and Johnson did not identify differences in sexual *desire* between men and women, but later studies have indicated that there are distinct differences in sexual desire between most men and women. While some couples report that they have similar levels of sexual interest and desire, many women report less of a biological drive motivating them to engage in sex. Rather, women may choose to engage in sex for the purpose of emotional and physical intimacy, knowing that they will get in the mood and enjoy the experience once they begin. Although spontaneous desire may be decreased at different times in life, staying open and receptive to a sexual experience for the purpose of closeness is likely to result in sexual arousal. Once sexually aroused, desire then kicks in, resulting in a potentially satisfying sexual experience. This reframing helps to alleviate anxiety in women who feel that their lack of spontaneous sexual desire is dysfunctional, and it normalizes their experience. Women should also be aware that men's sexuality is also rooted in their emotional, as well as physical, connection to their partners.

Furthermore, many women report that sexual desire peaks at various times throughout the monthly cycle. Fortunately, these peaks tend to correspond with sexually permissible times according to Jewish law. However, some women find that their desire peaks when they are in the *niddah* period, which may present a challenge to the couple. Because many factors may contribute to variations in desire, we recommend consulting a certified sex therapist.

CHAPTER 13
Male sexual desire

DESIRE AND AROUSAL occur when stimuli received through the senses activate emotional and physical responses. For most men, the sense of sight tends to be a primary initiator of sexual feelings, expectations and subsequent behaviors. Seeing your wife in alluring lingerie, or wrapped in a towel after a shower, or even in her sweat pants and t-shirt, are classic examples of that kind of sexual trigger. Other senses may also contribute to an intimate atmosphere, such as the aroma of her perfume or her stimulating touch. Women may respond in a similar way to sensory stimuli.

While studies indicate that men and women's sexual responses are equally intense, men seem to desire sex more frequently than women, throughout the life cycle and across cultures. Men are also motivated to engage in sex for the purpose of expressing intimacy and creating genuine connection, emotionally as well as physically. It is also important to note that while men's sexual desire may feel more prevailing, it is by no means an uncontrollable force, and there is a mutual expectation in a healthy marriage to regulate one's sex drive.

The intensity and frequency of desire are not only biologically determined, but are also influenced by cultural and familial values and expectations, and of course by opportunity. While these factors are important, they do not automatically weaken any man's capacity for empathy, understanding and self-control.

For observant people, sexual behavior is governed by permitted times and circumstances, and this often impacts on desire as well. Starting from puberty, men experience sexual desire, at times frequently. During this period, options to respond to these feelings through masturbation or partnered sexual activity remain outside of *halachic* expectations. As such, having these feelings, which are perfectly normal and natural, may engender guilt and shame. This issue is often made even more challenging as the secular world views premarital physical touch and masturbation as acceptable behaviors. This can be a truly trying time, and for those feeling overwhelmed by negative emotions regarding sexual urges, we strongly recommend speaking with a culturally sensitive therapist.

Jewish life values sexuality in the context of marriage. Once married and hopefully enjoying a healthy sex life, it is still necessary to work together to negotiate a mutually satisfying sex life. As we have noted earlier, the "two weeks on, two weeks off" rhythm of *taharat hamishpachah* requires that couples refrain from physical intimacy part of each month, to be rekindled on *mikveh* night. Dealing with desire during the off weeks may be particularly frustrating for both partners, while others may feel pressured to perform sexually only because the calendar gives renewed permission. In addition, when the wife is not a *niddah*, she may want to engage in sex when the husband is not in the mood, or she may not be available or interested in sex when he is. From our experience, most couples find a manageable balance, particularly when they have developed good communication, empathy and trust.

V. SEXUAL ENHANCEMENT

Although legality is of the essence, an ideal marriage is an unending courtship. No possessiveness. No taking for granted. The lover never acquires any possessive rights over the privacy and personhood of his beloved.

I N THIS SECTION, we will provide guidelines for a variety of sexual experiences you can share with each other. If you have read the previous chapters, you recognize the importance we place on the notions of mutual sensitivity, consent and sharing as critical foundations for an enjoyable sex life. Speak with each other before you try any of the following options, and don't expect to get it right the first time – practice and a sense of humor should put you on the right track. And if it hurts or feels uncomfortable, don't do it.

If any of these activities raise *halachic* questions for you, consult both a *halachic* authority (see chapter 7) and a certified sexual health professional in order to provide acceptable alternatives.

CHAPTER 14
Sensual touch and massage

I NTENSE INTIMATE EXPERIENCES need not be limited to the genitals. Wherever you have skin, you have nerve endings, and wherever you have nerve endings, tactile pleasure is possible. Giving each other massages can be educational as well as enjoyable; you have the opportunity to discover that enjoyment can come from body areas you may not have thought to be sensual.

Start experimenting with massages on non-intimate areas, gradually moving to more direct genital touch. Talk with each other, as the mutual feedback will guide you to the right place and the right motion. This should be a head-to-toe experience, so take your time. If you become aroused, then take this to wherever you both wish to go, although you may find that at times a massage by itself can be sufficiently satisfying.

Try massaging body lotion or oil on each other. This can be confined to a specific area, such as the back or legs. For a truly sensual experience, give each other a full body massage with a fragrant oil, safe for sensitive body parts. Start with more neutral sections – hands, feet – gradually ending with direct genital arousal. Finishing off with a shower together (see below) can make for a memorable evening.

Talk less, touch more – Sit on a bed or on the floor with the minimum amount of clothing in which you feel comfortable, or preferably none at all. Taking turns, each of you takes the hand of your partner and uses it to touch/caress/massage any area of your own body, as long as it is comfortable. Your partner's hand becomes your means to give yourself pleasure. Then switch. Talk with each other about what feels good, and don't worry about eye contact; some people like it, while others may not.

Showering – Another tactile experience which couples often enjoy is showering together. Assuming you have a shower big enough for the two of you to stand comfortably, bathing each other with soap and warm water, including slowly shampooing each other's hair, can be a genuinely sensuous experience. Before you start, make certain that you both agree on how and how much you wish to be touched, and be sensitive to each other's level of comfort as you continue. This is truly a full body experience.

An additional enhancement for these touch options is the use of candles. Using one or two scented candles anywhere in your home, instead of regular lighting, can turn an ordinary space into one of romance and excitement.

Hair – Taking the time to run your fingers through your partner's hair is a pleasant sensation for the two of you, and keeping your hair clean makes this an even more welcoming experience. If you have little or no hair on your head, a scalp massage can be equally satisfying.

Body hair, though, may present some challenges. Western culture assumes that women will regularly remove underarm hair and shave their legs, with men generally exempt from this effort.

For some of you, body hair may have no particular significance. In many cases, regular bathing and deodorant use may allow for more comfortable physical contact. Where this is not sufficient, consulting a sexual health professional and/or a dermatologist should be the next step.

Disrobing – If you have been married for a while, you may recall some of your initial hesitancy at being naked with your new spouse. For most couples, the anxiety associated with taking off all of your clothes, or having your partner take them off for you, passes rather quickly. However, each of you may have different comfort levels with nudity, attitudes which may be influenced by gender, body image, cultural norms and family values. This topic may be more complex for women, living in an era unduly influenced by media expectations of "ideal" female bodies, but men can be quite body-conscious as well. For both of you, though, the vicissitudes of life guarantee that your bodies will change as you age.

Despite these challenges, we encourage you to enhance your mutual comfort being naked with each other, and not only when sexual intercourse is the primary goal. Regardless of your shape and size, the more physically fit you are and the better you feel about your body, the more you will enjoy every aspect of your intimate lives. So, take care of yourselves and enjoy each other, especially when you remove your clothing.

Because of the exclusivity and privacy of your relationship, opportunities to be naked together will be limited. In that context, here are some suggestions:

We wrote earlier of the potential pleasure of showering together and that part of the enjoyment can be the freedom from clothing that you both can experience. On your way to and from the shower, try spending a few minutes in the space of your bedroom naked. If you would like to be a bit more adventurous, stand naked with your partner in front of a full-length mirror. Each of you, in turn, describes your body from head to toe out loud. This is intense and requires a significant level of trust. You can also try to sleep together naked.

Depending on your geographic area, you may be able to find a place to share a naked swim or, probably more readily available, a place to soak naked together in a hot tub. Just a word of warning – do not try to have intercourse while your genitals are submerged. The water can wash away natural vaginal lubrication and introduce water of questionable cleanliness into the vagina.

CHAPTER 15
Exploring sexual accessories

T OYS ARE NOT just for kids. The term "sexual aids" refers to objects that may be used to enhance your sexual pleasure. While a wide variety of devices are available, we will describe two of the commonly used aids, or toys as they are often called. With any sexual aid, wash it well after use with soap and warm water.

Penis rings

As described, an erection occurs when sexual stimuli trigger the brain to send signals to increase blood flow to the penis. Blood flows to organs through arteries, and away from organs, through veins. When arteries supply blood to the penis, the specialized penile tissue becomes filled with blood, and the penis hardens. When blood flows away from the penis through the veins, the hardening, or erection, is reduced.

The purpose of a penis ring is to create a situation where the blood can't escape the penile tissue as easily as it can enter it, resulting in some penises becoming slightly more filled with blood (and erect). With the additional blood flow, some men experience an increase in sensitivity throughout the penis. Assisting the penis in retaining its increased blood volume may help with "staying power." Keep in mind that everyone's body is different. Penis rings are safe if used properly, but should not be worn longer than 30 minutes.

There are two types of penis rings. One is designed to go around the base of the penis, resting on the underside between the shaft and the scrotum. The other design has the ring resting on the underside behind the scrotum, between the scrotum and perineum (the area between the scrotum and anus). Either type should be made of an elastic material – rubber, latex or silicone.

Vibrators

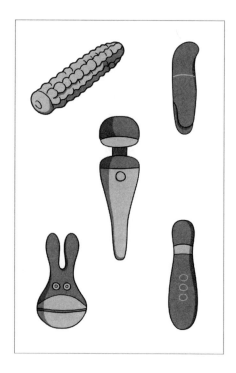

A vibrator is a sex toy that is used on the body to produce pleasurable erotic stimulation. Most vibrators contain an electric-powered device that pulsates or throbs, and can be used to stimulate erogenous zones such as the penis, clitoris, and the rest of the vulva or vagina. Vibrators may be recommended by sex therapists to women who have difficulty reaching orgasm through masturbation, partner's hand or mouth stimulation and/or intercourse.

As the above pictures illustrate, there are many different shapes and models of vibrators. Some vibrators run on batteries, while others have a power cord that plugs into a wall socket. Some are intended primarily for external clitoral stimulation while others can be inserted into the vagina. If you need guidance as to which is appropriate for you speak to a certified sexual health professional. Most vibrators fall into several broad categories:

- The clitoral vibrator is used to provide sexual pleasure and to enhance orgasm by stimulating the clitoris. Most of the vibrators available can be used as clitoral vibrators, and they commonly come in a variety of colors, textures and shapes.

- Penis-shaped vibrators can be made of plastic, silicone, rubber, vinyl, or latex, and are designed for both individual usage or with a partner. They come in different sizes, colors and textures.

- "The Rabbit" is a two-pronged device for simultaneous stimulation of both the vagina and the clitoris. The rabbit vibrator actually consists of two vibrators of different sizes. A penis-shaped vibrator is intended for insertion into the vagina to stimulate the vagina, while a smaller clitoral stimulator simultaneously touches the clitoris. The rabbit vibrator was named after the shape of the clitoral stimulator, which resembles a pair of rabbit ears. They are normally made of rubber, jelly, silicone, or latex and they come in a wide variety of colors, sizes and designs. If this vibrator does not provide simultaneous stimulation due to variations in women's anatomy, one may try using two different vibrators simultaneously.

Many women find direct clitoral stimulation with the vibrator to be too intense initially. Begin by using the vibrator on the abdomen and inner thighs, slowly working your way to the genitals, and eventually, moving directly to the clitoris. Some women enjoy inserting the vibrator into the vagina.

CHAPTER 16
Exploring sexual positions

MOST COUPLES MAKE use of a limited number of sexual positions during their married lives, and for many it is most comfortable to stick with one position. In this section, we will suggest some alternate positions, should you wish to add variety to your sexual repertoire. Here are a few pointers:

- There is no obligation to add to your sexual positions; if you are both happy with the positions you know, stick with them.

- Make sure you both are in agreement if you want to try something new.

- Any selection should take into consideration factors such as age, physical condition, flexibility and emotional comfort level.

- You may wish to rehearse a position with your clothes on, to understand how to arrange your body for the position.

- A new position may require some practice and experimentation before you make it your own. Give it some time and be prepared to laugh about your initial attempts.

Below you will find illustrations and descriptions of five sexual positions that we recommend based on their potential for enhancing your intimate pleasure and for ease of learning:

1. Male on Top, With Her Legs Pulled In

How to do it: When the man is in the on-top position, the woman lifts her feet off the bed and pulls her knees into her chest. The couple can get into this position while he's inside or before he penetrates. As he pushes in and out, she rocks her hips back and forth.

Variations to try: This position is a great example of the power of small changes. Even moving her legs closer to or further from her chest by a few inches will create a different angle of penetration and potentially greater pleasure for both of you. She can also pull her legs further apart or squeeze them closer together, or keep one foot flat on the bed and the other leg lifted into the air. If she is limber, she can also try resting both of her ankles on his shoulders.

2. Male on Top, With a Pillow Under Her Hips

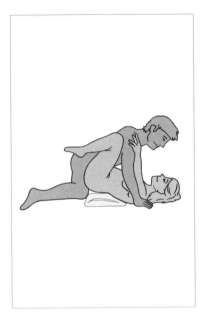

How to do it: Before the couple begins intercourse, she places a pillow under her hips, then he enters her as he normally does. This is an easy variation that can create pleasure-enhancing results for both of you. It helps his body push against her clitoris, which may help her reach orgasm. You can both focus more on grinding against each other instead of thrusting in and out.

3. Dangling Over the Edge of the Bed

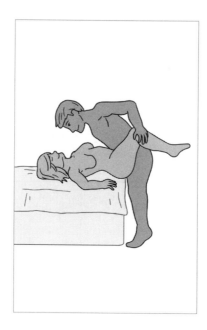

How to do it: She lies on her back with her legs hanging off the end of the bed. He places his body between her legs, enters her, and begins thrusting. This is an easy position for him because it doesn't require that he hold up his body weight with his arms.

Variations to try: If your bed isn't the correct height for your bodies to line up, you can try putting a pillow under her hips. Alternatively, he can kneel on the floor between her legs. He can hold each of her thighs in his arms for more leverage and intensity. She can also move her legs closer or further apart from each other, or she can rest her ankles on his shoulders for extremely deep and powerful penetration.

4. Woman on Top

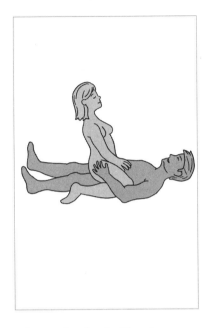

How to do it: He lies on his back. She sits on top of him, resting one leg on either side of his body. She slowly lowers her vagina down onto his erect penis. This can be an intense position to begin, so you may want to start with another position first, or use some additional lubricant. This position frees up your hands to caress each other and allows for more intimate eye contact.

Variations to try: She may experiment with a number of different ways of moving her hips. She can grind in a slow circle or push her hips towards and away from his chest. They can both move their hips up and down, and she can try changing the angle of her body by leaning forward or back, with either or both partners touching her clitoris. The couple should communicate about the best way for her to move her hips for maximal comfort and enjoyment for both.

5. On a Chair

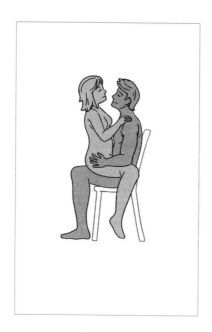

How to do it: He sits in a chair that is short and sturdy, without wheels. It is preferable to use something that doesn't have arm-rests, since they can get in the way. Facing him, she slowly lowers herself onto his lap and his penis. Both of her feet will be on the ground, or she can hold onto the back of the chair or his shoulders for additional support. She can easily move up and down, or she can grind her hips in a seductive circle or figure-eight pattern. His hands are free to hold or massage her.

Variations to try: The couple can employ this position on a sofa or on the bed against a headboard. He's still sitting up, but she is on her knees facing him. She can also try turning around and lowering herself onto him backwards, which will create an entirely new angle of penetration.

CHAPTER 17
Exploring sexual fantasies

T HE TOPIC OF sexual fantasies may cause some to feel uncomfortable. In truth, our fantasies can take us to places that our reality often seems to frown upon, places that may frighten us and tarnish our own self-image. Yet, all fantasies serve a purpose. For most of us, such mental depictions give enough of a sense of satisfaction that we will not act in a manner that might cause harm to ourselves or to others. Think of it as an emotional safety valve. Continually repressing our fantasies could result in frustration leading to out-of-control behavior.

Fantasies can provide direction for the enhancement of your sex lives. Research indicates that half of the population will feel comfortable sharing their fantasies with their partners, while the other half will prefer not to share them, and keep them private. If you would rather keep these images to yourself, you should never feel coerced to violate those boundaries. And of course, these feelings may change as your mutual trust becomes stronger.

If you choose to share your sexual fantasies with your spouse, here are some guidelines. Verbalizing your fantasies should never be taken as an implied invitation to put them into action. Feeling sufficiently trusting to reveal your inner worlds to each other is an emotionally intimate experience. In a similar vein, creating a fantasy together can be fun, and the content need not be totally beyond your reality. We are reminded of clients, parents of a large family, whose mutually-created fantasy consisted of being on a deserted island without their children. (Not hard to relate to, is it?)

Imagining the pleasure of a future event – also a kind of fantasy – can be warmly arousing and heighten the enjoyment of the actual event when it occurs. Think about the countdown until *mikveh* night or until a well-deserved weekend away.

For those of you who wish to take this further, fantasies can be a springboard for adding items to your sexual repertoire. Remember to fully discuss any new sexual behavior before attempting to put it into action, and expect to modify as you learn from this new experience. One direction this can take is role-playing, where each of you become characters in a scenario distant from your actual lives, for example doctor and patient, or singles tentatively exploring sex with each other for the first time, or photographer and model (just do not send any pictures to each other's phones!). One ultra-orthodox couple we know regretted never having had the experience of fooling around in the backseat of a car, so they rented a car, drove it to a secluded place and had a great time.

Chapter 18
Exploring oral lovemaking

Your lips are among the most sensitive areas of your bodies, providing additional opportunities for mutual enjoyment. Whether you have already become seasoned kissers or if your kissing has not been pleasing, here are some tips. For many, gentle kissing provides an especially sensual experience, no matter what shape your body is in. And while you may be most accustomed to giving or receiving kisses on lips or cheeks, any place you have skin works just fine.

Here are two kissing options you may wish to try:

- Start with gentle kisses on the nape of your partner's neck, then very slowly kiss up the neck, gently across the lips, and down the other side. Switch with your partner and repeat as often as it is enjoyable.

- Using tongues may be erotic or it may provoke some strong negative reactions. If you would like to give it a try, this is an easy first step – face each other, with one of you keeping your lips lightly closed; your partner gently darts tongue-touches from one end of your lips to the other and then back again. At first, do not prolong this too much. Stop if one of you is not pleased, but if you are both enjoying, talk about how to use your tongues for enhanced enjoyment.

Beyond kissing, lips and tongues can be part of even more intense sexual experiences, activities generally known as oral sex. While we will provide some specific guidelines, we encourage any reader who may have a *halachic* question to consult with a *halachic* authority familiar with the subject of physical intimacy. This is a sensitive, interactive behavior, and the chance of mutual pleasure is greatly enhanced if your communication is open, specific and sensitive to each other.

Oral sex generally refers to the woman using her lips and tongue to stimulate his penis, or the man using his lips and tongue to stimulate her vulva, vagina and/or clitoris. Receiving this kind of stimulation can bring both of you to orgasm. We emphasize again that no one should be coerced into trying this or any other sexual behavior. If, however, you are feeling adventurous, we offer some guidelines.

For men providing oral sex to their wives, the touch is usually using his mouth to stimulate her clitoris and vulvar lips. He can use his lips, but the preferable touch tends to be with the tongue. She can either be lying on her back, with his head between her legs, or he can be on his back and she can be on her knees on either side of his head and her vulva touching his mouth. Using his tongue and lips, he can explore which kind of oral touch she finds most enjoyable. We do not recommend beginning with placing the tongue directly on the clitoris. Rather, we suggest that he lick the immediate surrounding area first, particularly directly above the clitoris on the area known as the clitoral hood. Only when she is sufficiently aroused, should he directly lick the clitoris, as this area can be very sensitive.

If either of you initially find this sexual option to be overwhelming, you may want to try oral sex with her wearing underwear, thin cotton or possibly silk. This creates a potentially more comfortable barrier to direct touch, but can still afford her a tactile experience intense enough to provide maximum pleasure. This is also useful as a form of foreplay or warm-up toward other sexual activities.

For women orally stimulating their husbands, the arousal involves using her mouth to stimulate his penis and possibly his testicles. Contrary to popular belief, this version of oral sex does not necessarily involve taking his entire penis in her mouth. If having some of his penis in her mouth is not pleasant, she can provide stimulation by kissing or licking along the shaft (length) of his penis, and for some, particularly around the tip, which is often the most sensitive area. Here, too, starting on top of underwear may work for you.

If the woman does choose to place his penis in her mouth, the motion most often used is her sucking as much of his penis as is comfortable for her and provides stimulation for him. She can also put only a small part in her mouth, while at the same time using one of her hands to stimulate the rest of the length and/or his testicles (gently!).

Most couples find it most compatible for him to be lying on

his back and for her to find the most comfortable position. Think about trying various configurations for both of your bodies.

Oral sex also works well as foreplay, allowing for genital stimulation, which can lead, if you both wish, to intercourse and ejaculation into her vagina. It may take some practice for him to know when to ask her to stop oral stimulation in time to allow for penetration to occur in a manner comfortable for both of you.

VI. IN SICKNESS AND IN HEALTH: INTIMACY THROUGHOUT THE LIFE CYCLE

In Shir Hashirim (The Song of Songs) the beloved invites her lover to "his garden" to savor and enjoy; "Yavo dodi legano." Hence, the rabbinic rule: The Chatan (bridegroom) must not enter his chuppah, his love chamber, unless given permission by his kallah. She must first say "Yavo dodi legano."

CHAPTER 19
Pre-pregnancy considerations

B EFORE ADDRESSING PREGNANCY, it is important to acknowledge the pre-pregnancy periods in the couple's life. During your childbearing years, you are in one of three different states – either trying "not" to get pregnant, hoping and trying to get pregnant, or already expecting a child. All three of these situations have implications for your sex life.

Preventing pregnancy may affect a couple's sexual life, and fear of unwanted pregnancy may inhibit sexual desire and functioning. Barrier contraception methods, such as a diaphragm, may feel technical and affect spontaneity, as they often require interruption of sexual activity prior to intercourse. Hormonal birth control methods, such as oral contraceptives, may negatively affect a woman's sexual desire and response, and may contribute to vaginal dryness. Non-hormonal intrauterine devices such as an IUD are associated with additional menstrual bleeding, often extending the *niddah* period. Even natural methods (FAM – fertility awareness method) can affect sex by further restricting the days that a couple may engage in intercourse without contraception.

Many couples report that once they begin to attempt pregnancy, their sexual drive and function begin to increase. In women who have used oral contraception, this may be associated with resumption of ovulation and a normative hormonal milieu. This may also result from the motivation to create a baby together and to have fun trying. However, if a couple is challenged with infertility, this is likely to negatively affect their sex life.

Dealing with infertility increases stress for both partners. Fertility treatment is associated with exposure and lack of privacy, with lovemaking occurring according to instruction and often only at specific times. This can turn sexual relations into a chore, and couples may experience sex as technical and perfunctory. For men, the expectation of "on demand" ejaculation may engender erectile or ejaculation problems resulting from performance anxiety or exhaustion. Physically, hormone treatments can cause the female partner to feel pelvic tenderness, bloating and pain, and can affect her mood. Emotionally, couples are often challenged with mixed feelings including anxiety, failure, and even shame.

Chapter 20
Pregnancy

WHEN A WOMAN becomes pregnant, her sexuality and sexual relationship with her husband may be affected. Let's explore these changes by dividing the stages of pregnancy according to trimesters.

First Trimester

Although women are generally accustomed to bodily changes, including puberty, menstruation and ovulation, and later in life, menopause, pregnancy most significantly impacts the physical experience of a woman's body. As such, in the first trimester there may be a natural decrease in sexual desire.

Early pregnancy is often associated with fatigue, nausea, and breast tenderness, and these physical changes may inhibit sexual desire. There may be some mood swings and anxiety about becoming and staying pregnant. Additionally, one or both partners may be concerned about possibly harming the fetus or causing a miscarriage by engaging in penetrative sex.

For some couples, the initiation of pregnancy may bring differing expectations concerning sex. If a couple has been focused on successfully achieving a pregnancy, and sex had become conception-oriented, the couple may now be less motivated to engage sexually.

Since a pregnancy effectively removes the on/off rhythm of the *niddah* cycle, each partner may perceive this change differently. Without the clock of *niddah* ticking in the background, one partner may feel that the pressure has been removed while the other partner may wish to take more advantage of the extended time together.

Second Trimester

Many women report feeling better physically and emotionally in the second trimester, and as a result, sexual frequency may increase. From a physical perspective, there is usually a decrease in her nausea and fatigue. Vaginal blood flow increases significantly during pregnancy, and this process may result in increased sexual arousal and more orgasmic intensity. In fact, some women report that they first began experiencing orgasms during their first pregnancy.

From a psychological perspective, women often become more comfortable with their bodies as they begin to appear distinctly pregnant rather than merely "full." A woman's body image may improve due to breast enlargement or by simply feeling more confident as a pregnant woman and taking on that identity. Most men respond positively to their wives' changing body appearance, as they feel happiness and excitement about the impending birth. Observing the changes that a woman's body undergoes during pregnancy is often a source of awe, as well as humor, for many couples.

Third Trimester

In the third trimester, sexual intercourse may become more challenging. Many women suffer from numerous sources of discomfort related to pregnancy, including back and hip pain, varicose veins, urinary discomfort, hemorrhoids and heartburn.

The man-on-top position may be uncomfortable or even impossible due to the woman's growing abdomen and her difficulty lying on her back. Women may report pain due to intense uterine contractions, either when she reaches orgasm, or with male ejaculation, as chemicals known as prostaglandins in the semen can intensify uterine contractions. Vaginal lubrication at this stage may be somewhat reduced as blood flow is increased at the pelvic region rather than the vagina. Frequently, the muscles of the pelvic floor become weaker towards the end of pregnancy, which can affect both female and male arousal. Female arousal -as vaginal contractions are related to arousal and orgasmic intensity, and male arousal -as he may perceive less friction during intercourse. Some women experience urinary leakage that may inhibit them sexually.

It is important to note that expectant fathers may also experience changes that affect mood and sexual function. Concerns about harming the fetus, anxieties regarding fatherhood, and difficulty adjusting to change, may contribute to functional problems that can include reduced desire, erectile problems or premature or delayed ejaculation.

From a relational and socio-cultural perspective, the end of pregnancy may trigger some anxiety and disparate attitudes around sex, particularly in observant couples. While the female partner may be less comfortable physically, and experience less desire, often the male partner becomes anxious with the awareness that the postpartum period signifies a temporary cessation of sexual relations. Both partners may have concerns about new parenting roles and responsibilities.

As we noted earlier in this section, it is best to bring these challenges to the forefront and address them through communication.

Physical and emotional changes are normal and both partners should be encouraged to honestly and openly communicate their feelings to one another. Often, the couple is empowered to share deeper emotional intimacy during the first trimester, as many couples wait until the second trimester to reveal their status as parents-to-be. This, along with the shared excitement and expectation, often strengthens the bonds of intimacy.

A defining aspect of pregnancy is change and adjustment, and couples are advised to communicate their concerns and desires to one another. If one or both partners express fear that sexual activity may harm the fetus, it is important to consult with and receive reassurance from a physician. In most low-risk pregnancies, all sexual activity is completely safe, as the fetus is well protected within the confines of the surrounding membranes. Intercourse may be contraindicated when there is a history of premature delivery or when there is multiple gestation or other high-risk situations. In all cases, it is best to consult with your physician.

Adjustment may be required in both values and attitudes about sex, as well as in sexual activity. Couples should consider that hugging, kissing, massage and oral and manual stimulation are all legitimate and satisfying forms of physical intimacy, and that not all intimate and sexual situations must conclude with intercourse. Changes in sexual positions for intercourse should be considered as well. (See earlier for suggestions.)

Chapter 21
The postpartum period

T HE POSTPARTUM PERIOD is marked by significant change, not only physically, but also for the family and for society. The immediate postpartum period is generally one of mixed experiences that normally include happiness and euphoria, along with exhaustion, stress, anxiety, and in some cases, depression.

Physical symptoms during the postpartum period are related to recovery from the pregnancy and birth process, and to significant hormonal fluctuations. Both partners experience lack of sleep which impacts on their moods and day-to-day functioning, as well as on sexual desire. Physical symptoms may include body pain, genital and breast soreness, difficulty changing positions due to abdominal and pelvic floor weakness, and pelvic floor-related symptoms that may include urinary incontinence.

Emotionally, the postpartum woman may experience mood swings and may doubt her ability to care for her child. She may be attempting to process the birth experience as well, as she navigates attempting to take care of her own basic hygiene and nutrition while caring for others.

This is a particularly vulnerable period when couples often are challenged by the inability to provide one another with the most basic of human touch. Moreover, the physical distance that is created by the laws of *taharat hamishpachah* following birth affects each person differently. They may be unable to fall back on hugging to express apology, support or comfort. For this reason, improving verbal communication and providing emotional affirmation, validation, understanding and empathy, is crucial.

Although they are now parents, couples should continue to invest in their lives as husband and wife. Once it is time for *mikveh* immersion, there may be disparate expectations that relations resume after the *mikveh* exactly as before. Some women may not feel physically or emotionally ready for the resumption of sexual intercourse. They may, however, look forward to engaging physically or sexually in other ways. Again, open and honest communication is the key to navigating these challenging periods in a couple's intimate life.

Many couples are surprised that sexual relations may be subject to modification after childbirth. Male partners have often reported that they did not know or were not informed of this, and assumed that relations would resume as prior to childbirth, given only the cooperation of the baby.

Sexual life after childbirth, as in any stage of life and as mentioned previously, is affected by physical, psychological, relational and social factors. Desire for sex may decrease due to physiological factors, particularly in breastfeeding women. After childbirth, there is a dramatic decrease in estrogen and progesterone. Prolactin, which is secreted in order to stimulate the milk supply, decreases sexual drive. Lactating women often experience vaginal dryness that can inhibit desire and contribute to painful intercourse. Obstetrical stitches due to tearing or episiotomy may increase sensitivity and pain. Progesterone birth control pills, commonly used by nursing mothers, may also contribute to decreased desire. While hormonal birth control methods are common, women are often unaware that these methods reduce sexual drive. We suggest discussing alternate methods of birth control with your gynecologist.

Pelvic floor disorders, such as weakness, incontinence, prolapse and flatulence may be common after childbirth, and these contribute to inhibition and lack of desire to engage in sex. We recommend that in the weeks and months after childbirth, women seek a pelvic floor physical therapist to help alleviate childbirth-related pain and scarring, and strengthen the core muscles of the abdomen and pelvic floor.

Physical changes may affect a woman's body image and sense of herself as a sexual being. She may feel negative about the weight she has gained and how her body has changed. Conversely, she may enjoy her newer shape and fuller breasts, and this may facilitate her sex drive.

Women who are breastfeeding may feel inhibited by leaking breasts or by the perception that her breasts are now meant exclusively for the baby. The dual role of the breasts as providing bonding, attachment and nutrition to her infant, along with the sexual role, may feel confusing and dissonant for many men and women. It is not uncommon for some women to not want their husbands to touch their breasts while they are breastfeeding.

From a psychological perspective, research suggests that anywhere between 8%–20% of women suffer from postpartum depression, which may contribute to decreased sexual health. Moreover, antidepressant medication is likely to decrease her sexual desire and functioning as well.

The psychological experience of husbands transitioning into fatherhood may be equally complex. Fatherhood is a new world for men. Many new fathers experience anxiety, stress, and exhaustion, which may impact on their sexual desire and functioning. They may feel isolated or jealous of the mother-infant bond, and they may feel conflicted about initiating sex with their wife, or may fear causing her pain with intercourse.

Cuddling and caressing may provide physical connection without any performance expectations, and may give men as well as women the hope of a return to pre-baby sexual activities. And as all parents of newborns can attest, sometimes you just need to find a few moments to relax together.

On a relationship-dynamic level, it is important to acknowledge that the family system has changed, and the husband-wife dyad has now shifted to include another individual, one with many needs. For a man or woman taking care of a baby, and especially if there are other children, and even more so if their professional life is occupied with caring for others, either partner may perceive sex as a chore. Some women may view her partner's desire for sex as another physical need she must fulfill. In addition, much of the woman's needs for attachment and intimacy are fulfilled with her infant.

The following are suggestions for returning to physical and emotional intimacy after childbirth:

- Take care of yourself. Pay attention to your nutrition, try to get some exercise (even walking a few minutes each day), don't ignore health issues and make sure to sleep when you can.

- Take the time to reconnect to the world beyond your home. Be in touch with friends and family, and renew your interest in those activities that you enjoyed before this new stage of life.

- Share childcare responsibilities. This is a step in your re-connecting with each other. Sharing the moments of your baby's first milestones – smiling, laughing, or crawling – can create magical memories.

- Find ways to enhance your non-physical intimacy. This is especially important when either of you may feel isolated, sleep deprived and thoroughly wrung out. Take time to be kind to each other.

- When you know that your first postpartum *mikveh* night is coming up, share your feelings, expectations and desires. Take this slowly, doing your best to connect emotionally to each other as you again rejoin your intimate lives.

- You will need to rewrite your sexual script, taking into

consideration factors such as time restrictions, the presence of your baby in your bedroom and the possible physical and emotional effects of nursing.

- Babies seem to have a knack for crying while the two of you are "in the middle." To avoid this disconnect, both of you can get out of bed to tend to your child. If one of you is doing the feeding, your partner can gently give you a massage to maintain the intimacy of physical contact.

- As soon as you get the go-ahead from the pediatrician, move your baby out of your bedroom and return that space to its significance for you as a couple.

- If the situation seems to be spiraling out of control, get some help. This is a time when we all need support, so don't hesitate to ask for it.

And remember to maintain that important sense of humor.

CHAPTER 22
Intimacy at midlife and beyond

THE TRANSITIONS FROM the childbearing years to raising school-age and teenage children, marrying them off and becoming grandparents, present many developmental milestones. On an individual level, each of you continues to grow in your personal and professional lives, while as a couple you may experience deeper intimacy or instances of conflict. Major life events as well as normative daily struggles with children, employment, finances and health affect how we relate to one another as a couple. This affects your intimate lives as well.

For some couples, midlife challenges to intimacy include difficulty finding time and space in a home with older children wandering about at all hours. Resourceful couples may use the rare opportunities when no kids are around for a planned or spontaneous rendezvous, even if it is during the day.

Research indicates that predictors of maintaining and perpetuating a healthy and satisfactory sexual life after middle age include the shared attitude and value that sex is important and worth investing in, a history of satisfactory sex before midlife, and the blessing of good health. Other variables associated with maturity, including body acceptance, a more relaxed attitude, an empty nest and a relationship that represents years of shared emotional experiences, may result in your sexual lives improving over time.

Having said that, there are physical, psychological and relational factors that may affect a couple's sexual life as they age. As an example, for observant Jews for whom the menstrual cycle dictates the timing of intimate behaviors, the onset of menopause represents change. During the perimenopausal years, periods may be frequent and of longer duration, or random and unpredictable, which may become a source of stress. Communicating feelings to each other during these trying situations is of critical importance. The complete cessation of menstruation, which defines postmenopausal years, brings with it a novel freedom from concerns about birth control, *niddah* constraints, or ritual observances related to *taharat hamishpachah*. While some may miss this defining feature of Jewish sexual life, many couples welcome this new stage.

Menopause is also associated with physical symptoms that some women find distressful and uncomfortable. Declining levels of estrogen contribute to both physical and psychological symptoms. Physical symptoms may include hot flashes, night sweats, weight gain and bloating. Changes in the genitalia include decreased blood flow to the vagina and clitoris, as well as thinning of the mucosal lining of the vagina, resulting in dryness and atrophy. This may make intercourse feel uncomfortable or even painful, and using a lubricant may be extremely helpful.

As women age, the pelvic floor muscles that support the bladder, uterus and vagina becomes weakened, resulting in the dropping down and potential prolapse of one or more of those organs. Prolapse refers to the bladder, vagina, uterus and/or rectum descending down towards the vaginal canal. It may feel physically uncomfortable for either or both partners, and often affects a woman's body image. It is not unusual to experience urinary symptoms such as frequency and incontinence. Pelvic floor symptoms are associated with decreased sexual functioning and satisfaction. Pelvic floor exercises that strengthen muscles and help increase blood flow to the vagina and clitoris can help to improve sexual response. A pelvic floor physical therapist can be very useful in helping to strengthen the pelvic floor and alleviate these symptoms.

At middle age, it may take longer for a man or woman to become sexually aroused, it may take more time and effort to reach orgasm, and the intensity of the orgasm is sometimes decreased. It is important to be aware that for some women, the positive experience of sex is greatly increased through enhanced sensitivity and a deeper and more intense experience of orgasm.

Psychological reactions to menopause can include anxiety and depression, mood swings, fatigue, and sleeping difficulties. It is not unusual to experience decreased sexual desire.

Do not hesitate to discuss your physical, psychological and sexual responses with your doctor or sexual health professional. Some women benefit from hormonal therapy while for others this is not a desired or appropriate choice.

The changes that men undergo as they age have been referred to by some as andropause. A decline in male hormones may contribute to changes which affect health and sexual function. In men and women, hypertension, diabetes, chronic pain and arthritis may be conditions related to aging. Many systems of the body may be affected, including sexual functioning, due to decreased blood flow to the genital area.

Prostate conditions are common in men, and symptoms such as urinary frequency, difficulty urinating, and urethral burning may have both physical and psychological effects on sexual desire and function. Erectile difficulties and premature ejaculation are not uncommon.

In addition to difficulties in sexual function related to the genitalia, age-related systemic changes in both men and women will affect sex. As people age, they experience changes in sensation, and may no longer enjoy the type of touch they did in the past. Dry mouth may make kissing or oral sex difficult. Aches and pains and the overall decrease in endurance and mobility limit certain positions, and couples may need to "take a break" and catch their breath several times during sex.

The good news is that despite physical changes, studies show that as couples age, they can continue to engage in physical intimacy well into their golden years. According to a poll conducted in 2017, just over three-quarters of older adults in the United States think that sex is important for romantic relationships, no matter the age, and many agree that sex is important to their overall quality of life. Other studies on aging and sex, have noted that older couples report that sex is slower, more controlled, and less goal-oriented. As noted sex researcher Dr. Peggy Kleinplatz has stated, "optimal sexuality flourishes in the context of a relationship deepening with maturity."

CHAPTER 23
Intimacy and chronic illness

A S PEOPLE AGE, medical conditions, chronic illnesses or diseases often become a reality for one or both partners. While medical practitioners offer guidance and treatment for improving health and quality of life, questions regarding the effect of illness, medications and other treatments on sexual function are often not addressed.

The reasons for this are many, and include the fact that patients and their partners may be too embarrassed to ask about sex, or aren't sure that their practitioners are equipped to address these matters. Some physicians fail to ask about sexuality out of awkwardness, fear of embarrassing their patients, lack of knowledge in addressing the issues, or lack of awareness about their importance. Furthermore, they may assume that when faced with a diagnosis that may be life threatening, people are far more concerned with matters of life or death, rather than sex and intimacy.

In fact, many couples do cease sexual activity due to stress, exhaustion and illness, internalizing the message that they should consider themselves "lucky to be alive." However, studies indicate that when faced with their mortality, many people hold on to the desire to continue sexual activity as an affirmation of life. It is a way to feel normal when so much of life has changed. Engaging sexually with your partner, even when either of you faces disease or disability, is a way to continue to feel alive and vital.

There are many barriers to sexual intimacy on physical, psychological and relational levels, when dealing with illness. Common feelings for the patient include anxiety, depression, frustration, anger, lack of control and fear about an unknown future. The experience of being ill, including undergoing painful and/or intrusive procedures and treatments, may feel depersonalizing, and this may affect feelings towards one's self and body. After being poked and prodded, any kind of additional touch may feel uncomfortable or invasive. Patients may suffer from negative body image issue from weight gain or loss, scarring, or the removal of a body part. This may be particularly true in cases of alteration or removal of parts associated directly with sexuality, such as breast, uterus, ovaries or prostate. Illness may involve discharges, catheters and decreased control over body functioning, which can be a source of embarrassment and vulnerability.

Partners may also struggle with anxiety over the prospect of disability or death. They often become the caretaker and feel their own ambivalence about sex, whether feeling guilty for wanting to engage in sex, or for not feeling as attracted to their partner as they once felt.

On a physical level, many factors related both to the illness or disability and to the treatment might affect sexual functioning – fatigue, pain, stiffness and decreased mobility; side effects of medications, radiation and chemotherapy such as nausea, dry mouth and vaginal dryness or atrophy; lack of arousal or erectile dysfunction – can all affect sex. The illness or its treatment may affect blood flow, hormonal balance, nerve functioning, skin sensation or any of the other various systems of the body, thus impacting sexual function.

The best predictor of sexual satisfaction during and after illness is a satisfactory sexual relationship prior to illness. When both partners are motivated to continue to engage in sexual activity, communication, planning, the flexibility to try new and different activities and an open mind about ways to feel pleasure, are all very helpful.

Sexual health is part of overall health and well-being. Healthy eating, pain management, energy conservation including stress reduction and mindfulness, getting plenty of rest, as well as general and pelvic floor exercises will all be helpful in improving sexual functioning.

Consider re-eroticizing bedroom space that has become medicalized by covering medications with a blanket, and using clean and comfortable linens or satin sheets. Be open to non-demand activities such as massage, foreplay, and gentle genital touch. To increase sexual satisfaction, consider the use of a vibrator and lubricants.

If you are not up to having sex, discuss this openly and consider other options such as cuddling while watching a movie. The idea is that both partners feel able to connect, not out of guilt or sense of duty, but out of mutual desire to continue and affirm their love and devotion to one another, even in this challenging time of their lives.

Finally, raise questions about sexual health and functioning with your physician, and ask for information and resources that can be helpful to you in this meaningful part of your lives. Consulting with a sexual health professional with expertise in this area may be of great value as well.

VII. COUPLE DYNAMICS IN AND OUT OF THE BEDROOM

We pray that God will bring joy to the groom AND *to the bride, each as a person, and to the groom* WITH *the bride, both as a unified couple. The two can become a rejoicing unit only when each remains a rejoicing individual. No surrender, no conquest, no symbiosis. The couple must learn to live together, but also to leave space for one another.*

S EVERAL FACTORS MAY contribute to sexual problems. In addition to a dysfunction of biological systems or the effect of medications, sexual function may be affected by psychological conflicts, mood, lack of desire, relationship issues, lack of education, and negative cultural messages about sex.

The paradigm of addressing these seemingly diverse influences on sexual function is known as the biopsychosocial model.

This model recognizes that several factors may contribute to sexual difficulties in marriage. On a biological level, hormonal changes, illness, medications, pain in the genital area, or decreased blood flow to the genitals, can affect sexual function in men and women. On a psychological level, stress, guilt and conflict around sex, depression or anxiety may affect sexual desire and arousal. A lack of relationship satisfaction and marital struggles certainly may influence the desire to engage intimately.

Couples seeking sex therapy often indicate a problem with sexual function, such as rapid ejaculation, a lack of sexual desire by one of the partners, or a problem with sexual arousal, as the issue they bring to therapy. They frequently look for a behavioral solution, perhaps hormone treatments, exercises, sex toys or a libido-boosting pill that can "fix" the problem for the low-desire partner.

Traditional sex therapy interventions may offer the above exercises and techniques in order to address these functional issues. However, in many cases, couples end up feeling frustrated in the process. The same dynamics that occur in the marriage – for example one partner pursues and the other distances – may then be played out around the exercise interventions. Simply providing exercises and techniques to couples will not work if the underlying dynamics are not addressed.

Sexual problems in couples rarely exist simply because of an isolated physiological cause.

While physical issues should be identified and treated, it is important that marital dynamics be explored, as they are likely to impact the sexual life of a couple. In addition, there may be individual factors that need to be acknowledged and processed in a couple therapy setting. This could include one partner's struggle with an anxiety disorder, depression, or even the death of a parent. A history of abuse and trauma must also be explored.

CHAPTER 24
Vignettes

IN THIS CHAPTER, we will explore five common sexual situations that we see in our clinics, and illustrate them with examples:

1: Differences in desire

While women are frequently identified as the partners with less desire, the male partner may be less available or willing to engage in sexual relations. At times, each partner may attribute lower desire to the other. And while it is tempting to blame this on poor timing, there may be a power struggle at play that should be examined in the context of couple/sex therapy.

Many factors can contribute to low desire. Hormonal changes can affect libido, particularly after childbirth or related to aging, as can other medical issues such as chronic illness, or certain medications and treatments. However, when couples describe discrepancies in desire, more often than not, it is the couple's dynamic that needs to be addressed. The following case study illustrates this:

Ari and Ilana (names have been changed) are a busy professional couple in their forties. When presenting for therapy together, Ilana related feeling distressed in the marriage. "Ari is being mean and distant, and acting like a child. He walks around angry all the time, and nothing I do or say seems right. I don't feel close to him anymore."

Ari was angry and sarcastic. "Maybe if you would want to have sex more than once a month, it would help me feel closer."

Ilana quickly became reactive. "That is so not true and you know it! I OFFERED plenty of times and you were too busy with your computer games!"

"Right," responded Ari, "like you really meant it. I don't need your favors."

Ari and Ilana, both feeling lonely and hurt, had fallen into a mutually destructive pattern. They blamed, criticized, devalued, and injured one another constantly. This dynamic, together with navigating the stress of their jobs and raising four children, was creating a marriage that held little positive vitality. This dynamic contributed to little interest in sex for Ilana, and resulted in frustration and anger for Ari. Neither partner felt heard or understood.

Several months of therapy focused on recognizing how Ari and Ilana's way of communicating triggered one another in their most vulnerable places. As the daughter of two highly successful professionals, Ilana was held to high standards of academic performance as a child, and recalled that less-than-perfect scholastic achievements resulted in her parents' expression of deep disappointment. Through the therapy process, she was able to recognize that hearing criticism felt equal to feeling undervalued, unloved and simply "not good enough." These feelings were also intertwined with the guilt she felt about not studying hard enough, and disappointing her parents. Her experience of guilt was further exacerbated when Ari expressed frustration about not having sex. Because she felt so guilty about her lack of desire, she became defensive every time Ari brought up the subject.

Ari, who was raised in a large family, recalled the feelings of coming home from school unrecognized while his mother was busy with his four younger siblings. This feeling emerged frequently when arriving home from work without being greeted by his current family members. Furthermore, when Ilana was distant and avoidant, which she often was in order to avoid sex, Ari's loneliness and need for attention surfaced.

In the therapy process, Ari and Ilana began to understand each other's triggers, and soon began to communicate to one another with more honesty and vulnerability. Ari recognized that his frequent sarcasm was simply a defense mechanism he employed to protect himself from feeling rejected, and Ilana recognized that she did avoid both emotional and physical intimacy. Learning to communicate without triggering one another allowed Ilana to talk about how she had come to feel that sex was just another chore she had to fulfill to keep Ari happy, much like the responsibility she felt to her parents, to maintain academic performance. When she was simply too tired or stressed at the end of a long day, she felt guilty for not wanting sex, such that rather than providing empathy to

Ari, she became avoidant and distant. Even when she did feel like hugging or cuddling with Ari, she refrained from touching him, for fear that this would be construed as an invitation for sex.

Ari was able to communicate to Ilana that when they engaged in physical intimacy, he felt that he mattered to her. Ilana was able to recognize when she felt criticized and when she became defensive. More importantly, Ari and Ilana learned to communicate their feelings to one another without hurting each other. They learned to call a timeout when they felt reactive during an argument, and to meet again when they both felt calmer, to discuss the issue. They learned to use 'I feel' statements, rather than blaming and criticizing, which simply provoked defensive reactions. They learned to listen and reflect each on each other's statements, and to provide empathy to one another.

Ari and Ilana also began to view sex not only as an act that they did, but also as energy between them. They began to affirm and validate each other, to spontaneously do nice things for one another, send flirtatious text messages to each other, and spend more quality time together. Once Ilana realized that physical contact did not always have to lead to sex, she allowed herself to initiate more physical affection and hugs regularly. The atmosphere of intimacy, vulnerability, honesty, closeness and mutual acceptance, allowed Ilana to become more direct with Ari, and for the first time, to share with him what she felt was missing in their sex life, and what she would like to experience. At this point Ari and Ilana's sex life improved dramatically.

2: When your spouse has experienced trauma or abuse

Couples may suffer from sexual difficulties that result from one (or both) of the partner's past history of trauma or abuse. Abuse affects the ability to engage in healthy intimacy. Abuse negatively affects emotional development and a healthy sense of self. Without a strong sense of self, individuals lack feelings of autonomy and control, as well as the ability to verbalize their boundaries, their feelings, and their desires. People who have been abused may not be able to enjoy the sensations associated with sex due to conflicted feelings of guilt and shame, and the triggering of pleasurable sensations associated with abuse. At times, they may disconnect or disassociate during sex by engaging in the act, but not staying emotionally present.

If you discover that your partner has been abused, he or she will need to initially undergo individual therapy to process the abuse, and couple/sex therapy may also be necessary. Standard sex therapy techniques, which provide gradual exposure to touch may need to be modified, as the partner who has been traumatized by abuse may become easily triggered and lose his/her feeling of safety and security. Sexual arousal may be triggering as well, and may trigger flashbacks and emotional disconnection from the experience. Sexual arousal may become connected with fear, horror and guilt, and once that connection is made, it is difficult to separate those experiences in normative sexual situations. This is distressing for both partners. Therapy can help the couple create a safe and healthy sexual narrative for the abused partner.

It is important to note that many people suffer from non-sexually related trauma that impacts emotional and physical intimacy. Post-traumatic stress disorder, or PTSD, is a serious condition that can affect individuals after being directly or indirectly exposed to a traumatic, life-threatening event. The symptoms of PTSD are intrusive. They include flashbacks, nightmares, and difficulties with concentration and sleep. People with PTSD tend to easily become anxious and irritated. Because they are easily triggered, they may avoid crowds or overly stimulating events. PTSD symptoms impact not only quality of life and sense of self, but also the individual's social, recreational and occupational lives.

Although only a small percentage of people who experience a trauma will go on to develop the symptoms of PTSD, there appears to be increasing awareness about this condition among mental health professionals as well as the general population.

Individuals who have been traumatized are wired to be alert and hypervigilant. They often cannot easily regulate their emotions and they can become agitated and even aggressive. They have an exaggerated startle response, such that a partner's reaching out with an intimate gesture can result in a hyper-reactive and rejecting response. Sexual intimacy requires feelings of safety, emotional and physical vulnerability, connectedness and the ability to let go – states which are difficult for trauma survivors to attain. The following case illustrates this:

Baruch, recently married to Shira, is a 23-year-old combat sol-
dier who served in the Israeli army. In the course of a mission,
enemy fire injured three men in his battalion and two were killed.
Baruch, who was inside his tank, was physically unharmed, but
the impact of the terrifying incident affected him intensely and he
suffered from severe anxiety, flashbacks, nightmares, and difficulty
sleeping. After six months, Baruch was diagnosed with PTSD.
He underwent a year of intense therapy that helped him learn
to recognize his triggers, self-soothe, and keep calm in stressful
situations. He was taking medication to help with depression and
anxiety and was also exercising regularly.

Shira came with him to couple therapy, stating that while Baruch
was much improved, he was difficult to live with. He often became
aggressive with her and avoided emotional or physical intimacy.
When they did have sex, he would either not be able to get an
erection, or become very quickly aroused and ejaculate quickly,
often before intercourse.

Therapy for Baruch and Shira included psychoeducation based on
explaining to them exactly how his trauma affects sex. Sexual de-
sire involves parts of the brain and release of brain chemicals that
are similar to those involved in the stress response. Our excitatory
mechanisms cause the heart rate to increase and the blood to flow
but our inhibitory centers let us know that even though our body is
in a state similar to the flight or fight response, we have nothing to
fear. People with PTSD lack that regulation. Once they experience
sensations and a physiological reality that mirrors stress, they may

experience a heightened fear response. Because Baruch experienced these responses, he was holding back from allowing himself to become aroused, which accounted for his erectile dysfunction. On other occasions when he would become aroused quickly and ejaculate just as quickly, he reported that he didn't feel anything. We understood that Baruch was simply disassociating from the act, though physiologically, his body was responding.

In the course of therapy, it also became apparent that Shira was eager to become pregnant, and this was an additional source of stress for Baruch.

Treatment for Baruch and Shira allowed each of them to better communicate their feelings in the marriage, to foster improved understanding of one another, and to create opportunities to increase emotional intimacy with compassion and empathy. The sex therapy component was focused on restoring awareness of sensations and the experience of pleasure without demands on performance. After several months of therapy, while Baruch still suffered from the aftereffects of his experiences in combat, he and Shira were able to recreate the intimacy that had been lost and enjoyed making love, not war.

3: When sex feels like a chore

In Judaism, marriage partners are encouraged to develop their sexuality together, while building an exclusive, intimate bond.

While typically, sexual education is very limited in Orthodox communities, premarital counselors often provide basic information and set the tone for the development of marital sexual values. Premarital guidance varies across communities. Some educators emphasize the Torah obligation for a man to satisfy his wife, and some *kallah* teachers underscore the importance of women being always available to their husbands.

This message, sometimes implied and sometimes directly stated, directs women towards sexual availability in order that their husbands avoid a nocturnal emission, masturbation or possibly looking outside the marriage for a sexual experience. In some communities, women are taught that they are not allowed to directly refuse sex when approached by their husbands. This model may be based on the assumption that both partners in principle enjoy sexual activity such that when there is sensitivity and good will, there exists the motivation to fulfill one another's desires even when one partner may be less interested. Moreover, when partners are sensitive to each other, they would naturally refrain from initiating sex when the other spouse is uninterested, tired or not feeling well. However, difficulties develop when there is a disparity in sexual interest, a lack of sexual enjoyment, or the experience of anxiety or pain with intercourse. In these cases, when a woman is expected to be available for sex despite the aforementioned situations, she will perceive herself as being taken for granted, or worse, as an object to fulfill and contain her husband's sexual desires.

When sexual intercourse is desired and pleasurable for both partners, the need for intra-vaginal ejaculation to occur as part of the sexual relationship may not present a specific difficulty. However, when the woman does not find sexual intercourse to be enjoyable or satisfying, the expectation that she function sexually as a fulfillment of marital responsibility may foster feelings of objectification and lack of autonomy. Moreover, this becomes more problematic when the woman experiences sexual pain.

The laws of *taharat hamishpachah* may also contribute to feelings of sex as a chore, particularly on *Mikveh* night or at the end of the permitted period, when time for sex is near its end. Conversely, while some women value the cycle of sexual abstinence and renewal, life cycle realities such as pregnancy, breastfeeding and menopause do not offer an abstinence cycle, making constant "availability" feel overwhelming.

Despite the Biblical and rabbinic injunction that it is the man's responsibility to provide his wife with intimacy, a married woman may feel obligated to engage in intercourse in order to fulfill her husband's needs. In a 2009 published study on Orthodox Jewish women and sexual life, co-authored by one of the authors of this book (TR), Orthodox Jewish women reported decreased physical satisfaction, yet greater overall sexual frequency compared with that reported by their secular counterparts, suggesting that some Orthodox women may in fact view sexual relations as their obligation. The following vignettes illustrate this experience:

"Sometimes after a long day with the kids and working, I am just so tired. I am afraid he will ask to be together and if he does, you are really not allowed to say no. Since I'm nursing, I feel dry and intercourse is painful. I really wouldn't mind just doing it with my hand, but I know that isn't allowed."

"When my husband was learning in the Kollel, my Kallah teacher told me we should do it twice a week, which was OK. Now he has a job and she says that since he sees women at work, this makes him have a greater Yetzer (desire), so we should have relations more frequently. Since I am in my eighth month and already have two little kids, this can get very difficult. But what can I do? I wouldn't want him to have a kishalon (failure) because of me."

"I know that on Mikveh night I am supposed to want to have sex, but after two weeks of no physical contact, I really need some time to get used to it again. I wish we could cuddle and take our time, but he gets so excited so quickly that we have to have intercourse before I am ready. He feels really bad about it. He wants us to take our time but then he can't help it because he hasn't ejaculated in two weeks. I feel like I have to be his vessel."

In these examples, we focused on the perspective of women, since in our clinical experience they express the feeling of sex as a chore more frequently than men. Some husbands, however, have similar emotional responses, but may be reluctant to give voice to them, not wanting to be perceived as less than manly. As one example, for couples with fertility issues, scheduled sex during ovulation may be a suggested treatment, demanding a husband's sexual performance – erection and ejaculation – at times when he may feel little or no sexual desire. Further along in the life cycle, postmenopausal women no longer concerned with challenges of *taharat hamishpachah* or birth control may experience a sexual renewal, and expect their no-longer-young husbands to exhibit equal interest and availability.

Rather than view sexual relations as an expression of mutual love and satisfaction, the above narratives describe viewing sex as a chore. These issues can be addressed with a combination of couple and sex therapy as well as consultation with a *halachic* authority who is understanding and sensitive.

4: Performance anxiety

The very expression, "sexual performance," conveys a message that for some men physical intimacy looms as a constant challenge and that failure to perform makes a man less than masculine. As author and sex therapist Marty Klein has poignantly noted: "[Men] learn from an early age that manhood is conditional rather than absolute.... Not making the team, not being willing to fight, not performing in bed, losing a job – that's all it takes and our man no longer believes he is a man."

The expectation of performance may include having and maintaining an erection, succeeding at penetration, vaginal ejaculation, extended intercourse and/or assuring his wife's orgasm.

All of these imply the need to take an active role in achieving some goal, rather than simply enjoying the physical component of a loving relationship. The emotional weight of these expectations can at times impact negatively on the physical capacity to function sexually. Simply put, worry may overwhelm desire and arousal. This phenomenon is known as "performance anxiety," and we have found it particularly problematic among newlywed young men with no previous partnered sexual experience and little accurate sexual information. In this situation, consulting with a certified sexual health professional is recommended.

While problems with sexual functioning may be the result of various physical and emotional factors, we wish to highlight one other pervasive concern related to performance anxiety. As we age, sexual responses reflect changes resulting from the diminishing efficiency of various physical systems. For men, this may create a damaging cycle – as sexual responses weaken or slow down, anxiety about these changes may further interfere with a man's ability to fulfill his expectations or those of his partner. The following case illustrates this situation:

> Asher, a 63-year-old widower, had been married for 35 years before the death of his wife several years earlier. About six months ago he met Becky, a 59-year-old widow, at the Shabbat table of mutual friends. They have been dating for four months and are seriously considering marriage in the near future.
>
> Asher scheduled a session with a sex therapist because of his concerns about engaging in sexual relations once he and Becky wed.

During his intake session, Asher reported that his sex life with his first wife had generally been good and that sex had been comfortable and satisfying to both. As he has gotten older, Asher said he no longer experienced morning arousal or ejaculation during his sleep and had not felt any need of masturbation. In addition, Asher was taking medication for marginal high blood pressure and was trying to lose 15 pounds that he had gained over the years.

When the therapist asked if Asher had raised these issues with Becky, he replied that they had avoided the topic, and besides, when he was engaged to his first wife, it was considered inappropriate to speak with each other about intimate matters before marriage. He said he did find Becky to be attractive and could envision them enjoying each other physically. He just wanted some assurance that he could "function as a man" and not be the cause of disappointment.

After a full intake process, and discovering no other relevant factors, the therapist referred Asher to a physician to determine if any medical or medicine factors would interfere with Asher's sexual capacity. After receiving his permission, the therapist spoke with Asher's physician regarding the possible use of a medication to assist with erection (e.g., Viagra), should it be needed.

With Asher's consent, the therapist invited Becky to come in for a joint session, with some initial time spent alone with the therapist. Speaking with the therapist alone, Becky said her sex life during her first marriage had rarely been satisfying to her. Her husband never quite figured out how to help her reach orgasm, which she did primarily by herself. She was looking forward to a new chance at marital intimacy with Asher, but confessed to some anxiety and uncertainty as to what to expect. Due to her late husband's illness, they rarely had sex in the last several years of his life. In the period since his death, she completed menopause, and felt that she may have difficulty with intercourse after so many years of sexual inactivity.

The therapist suggested a short-term pre-marital treatment contract, to which the couple agreed. Over the course of several sessions, the therapist emphasized the importance of investing in their emotional intimacy as a basis for any physical interaction. They were encouraged to communicate openly with one another about their expectations, fears and concerns, and to stay curious with one another in order to learn about each other's desires.

The therapist helped them with strengthening their mutual trust to allow for greater security in talking with each other about sex. Work in this area enabled them to share their hesitancy about starting over with a new partner and to reach an initial level of understanding about expectations, starting with their wedding night. The therapist also explained the changes aging may cause in all aspects of human sexuality, from arousal through physical response.

Both partners were relieved to learn that they could focus on pleasure rather than performance. In addition, the couple learned about expanding their sexual repertoire beyond intercourse into other options for mutual pleasure. They were also given guidance and direction for moving towards intercourse if they so desired. For Asher, this included healthy lifestyle changes, exercise and medication to help him achieve erection. At the final session, the therapist suggested that they return for follow-up a month after the wedding.

5: Communication when intercourse is painful

Leah is a 32-year-old mother of two children. She and her husband, Josh, turned to therapy after the birth of their second child. Leah reported loss of desire and painful intercourse. Leah had never really enjoyed intercourse, but since this birth it had become painful. Leah had been to different therapists on her own, figuring this was "her issue." She had tried creams, lubricants, dilators and pelvic floor exercises. Leah felt guilty about not wanting to have sex and Josh was frustrated and angry. "She never lets me touch her anymore."

Since Leah reported not enjoying intercourse, the therapist asked Leah what she did enjoy, sexually. Leah reported that in the past, she had considered herself to be very sexual. She enjoyed cuddling, receiving massages that could turn into something more, and long passionate kisses. When the therapist asked Leah why they don't do that anymore, Leah said, "because it always leads to intercourse." When the therapist turned to Josh, he seemed surprised. As it turned out, Josh was more than willing to be intimate with

Leah in other ways without having to end in intercourse. Leah had been feeling so guilty about "denying" Josh, that she ignored how much she was denying herself. Once intercourse was off the table, Josh and Leah become much more intimate and passionate. They attempted intercourse again only after Leah felt truly aroused and ready, and by then, she began to enjoy the experience.

Society perpetuates perceptions that sexual touch has to end in intercourse. Women deny their own needs for affection, a hug, or any touch, because they don't want to "tease" their partners or "start what they can't finish." Many women who have pain with intercourse can continue to enjoy physical intimacy in other ways, but often feel guilty about it. However, women suffering from painful intercourse should consider that they neither asked to have this condition nor does it define them as sexually dysfunctional. Couples should understand that sexual pain affects them both, and is not the fault or responsibility of the women who experience pain.

Although the above vignette describes this issue from a female perspective, men may also desire to have intimate experiences without needing to "go all the way." Whether due to exhaustion, worry, illness, performance anxiety or other causal factors, men would also be comforted by the knowledge that they can be freed from the macho expectation – their own or their partner's – that intercourse must be the goal of every intimate contact. Men also like to be hugged, and may benefit from spousal or therapeutic support in order to express this aspect of their sexuality.

VIII. PASSIONATE MONOGAMY

Ani Ledodi Vedodi Li does not mean possession. It truly means: "I am for my lover and my lover is for me." They never acquire, possess or belong to each other. But they yearn to be with each other and live for each other.

T HE EXPECTATION FOR sexual exclusivity is a core value in Jewish marriage. However, in the current cultural climate, the value and meaning of monogamy is changing. According to some sex and marital therapists, the expectation for long-term monogamy is unrealistic and therefore people, seeking novelty and mystery, look outside the marriage. These experts recommend negotiating monogamy expectations and contracts, and have even coined a new status, "monogamish."

Esther Perel, author of *Mating in Captivity,* and *The State of Affairs: Rethinking Infidelity* suggests that "too much intimacy" in marriage can contribute to affairs by decreasing passion in married couples over time. It is the expectation of marriage partners to fulfill multiple roles, acting as best friends, co-parents, and lovers, which can undermine the erotic energy needed to create sexual desire. "After all," says Perel, "how can you desire what you already know you have?"

We wish to offer a different viewpoint that challenges this perspective.

We believe that it is precisely the experience of intimacy that can create, not destroy, passion. Intimacy creates the security necessary to allow for the vulnerability required to feel safe and free, sexually. Creating passion while experiencing deep intimacy, as well as a mutual commitment to the expectation of sexual exclusivity, are central to maintaining monogamy.

Nonetheless, we recognize the challenges involved in maintaining monogamy over the long term even among observant couples. We have, therefore, provided tools for navigating the preservation of a long term, committed, monogamous marriage. The following section addresses situations that endanger the stability of your relationship.

CHAPTER 25
Pornography and your marriage

T HE SEXUAL MESSAGES that permeate contemporary society have impacted every community, including our own. People confront sexual images and messages on a daily basis. Compounding this situation is unprecedented access to this material provided by the electronic world in which we live. We may not know the cumulative impact of these inputs, but we do know that we confront one particular phenomenon that may be relevant to you as a couple.

Perhaps no marital issue engenders stronger negative feelings than the topic of pornography. Discovering that a spouse has been viewing or reading pornographic material may often be perceived as an act of infidelity or an indication of sexual perversity. Reactions may range from bewilderment, fear and anger, to a decision to move toward divorce. Compounding this situation are conflicting and confusing messages as to the possible consequences of pornography entering the couple's dynamic.

In this section, we hope to offer some clarity to this complex situation and provide guidelines to assist you if this issue challenges your marriage. We strongly suggest that you not perceive pornography as a permanent stain on your relationship, but rather as a sign that a conflict exists and needs your full attention. While research indicates that growing numbers of women view or read pornographic material, men remain the primary consumers, particularly among religious couples, and therefore we will use male pronouns in this discussion. Our focus is that of sex therapists – we seek to enhance your understanding and give you tools to re-balance your lives together.

The lack of a clear, universally accepted definition of pornography confronts everyone who deals with this area. This may prove particularly relevant when spouses disagree as to whether potentially problematic material is perceived as pornographic. For example, what is the status of a lingerie advertisement? We suggest that for the purpose of clear communication, couples should adopt a perspective that is non-coercive and consensual. If either one of you thinks something is pornographic, your partner should not try to convince you otherwise.

Some couples, even religious ones, may not consider a partner's occasional pornography viewing a problem. However, the emotional impact of the discovery of a spouse's pornography viewing may have more than one manifestation for the partner confronted by this unanticipated behavior. Reactions may vary among couples, but we will identify several as particularly challenging to the marriage.

Perhaps most common is a sense of betrayal. The husband has brought something foreign and perceived as unclean into this most private marital area. Wives may fear that their husband's fantasies may have been focused elsewhere during the couple's sexual times together, possibly on sexual behaviors not considered to be religiously or culturally normative.

Secondly, the expectation of mutual trust may no longer exist since a secret has now been revealed, where none was ever suspected. Women have told us that discovering their spouse's secret pornography use has been the most painful aspect of this experience; had their husbands shared this struggle with them, the damage to the relationship might have been minimal or avoided entirely.

Additionally, men may wish to introduce images gained from Internet sites into the marital bed. Their requests or demands of their wives may cause these women to feel uncomfortable, embarrassed, and inadequate sexually or the object of their husband's control. Saying "yes" may diminish their sense of self-worth, and saying "no" may cause conflict.

Finally, some women have spoken of feeling that their expectations regarding a level of family spirituality have been tarnished, because pornographic material has entered their homes and because their ostensibly religious husbands are not as they seem.

For many of those who see themselves as betrayed by spousal pornography use, the response has been a reactive distancing from their husbands. This need for space can be physical, emotional or both, and may be a necessary stage before healing can occur. As therapists, we emphasize the critical importance of communicating, particularly of listening, as an initial step in any attempt of two people to regain some balance in their relationship. This requires the husband to listen to the painful emotions his spouse now experiences. It likewise requires her to listen and attempt to understand the motivations for his behavior, and the meaning pornography holds for him.

To assist spouses in gaining some insight into reasons for pornographic use, we offer the following potential motivations:

Many men use this material as a means to transport themselves to a fantasy world, which is stress-free with seemingly no negative consequences and with no performance expectations. They are not expected to initiate, to perform, to worry about satisfying their partner or to contend with feelings of rejection. This stress-free zone may indeed be calming and allow for a sense of control away from a real world perceived as conflictual and beyond control. In fact, many of us use similar mechanisms when we read fiction or watch movies. The added sexual dimension inherent in pornography makes this escape choice explosive, and likely brings with it the consequences we have discussed.

A lack of satisfaction, sexually, emotionally, spiritually or otherwise is also a common motivator. Some men indicate a general absence of vitality and satisfaction in their marital sex life. They may feel restricted by a wife's reluctance to engage in sexual activities not acceptable to her. These feelings are often accompanied by a belief that no improvement is on the horizon. Dealing with this level of frustration by seeking a sexual outlet via pornography may seem preferable to confronting and attempting to resolve conflicts.

If this issue challenges you within your marriage, seek professional help as soon as possible. Find a certified sex therapist, and stay away from using labels such as "sex addict" or "sexual pervert" and from advisors or counselors who make use of such labels. Like other issues that may plague a marriage, pornography can create a sense of hopelessness and helplessness. We encourage you to re-invest in each other, and with guidance, to rediscover that place of trust and fulfillment.

CHAPTER 26
Infidelity: meaning and healing

S EXUAL EXCLUSIVITY IS a core value of Jewish marriage. Extramarital sexual contact –infidelity – represents not only a breach of Jewish law, but also a rupture of the couple's loyalty and trust. Whether you are seriously considering having an affair, are currently involved in undiscovered extramarital behavior, or your spouse has disclosed participation in an extramarital affair, there is cause for therapeutic intervention. In this section, we discuss the definition of infidelity, the possible reasons why partners may seek to engage in sexual behavior outside marriage, and some of the steps towards recovery and reconnection.

What constitutes infidelity? The definition of those behaviors and actions considered a betrayal is subjective and culturally defined. In our evolving electronic universe, where one can easily move from a public Facebook conversation to a private Messenger communication, couples need to have a sense of the type of boundaries with which they are comfortable regarding outside contacts. Spouses should discuss and agree on what feels right for them. Much of this comfort level is based on trust, communal norms, and how each couple themselves negotiates what constitutes acceptable or unacceptable behaviors. For example, some couples may consider masturbation or viewing pornography as a marital betrayal.

While a WhatsApp conversation or a business lunch with a member of the opposite sex may be completely appropriate, if you find yourself quickly deleting texts or purposely omitting the mention of lunch meetings with a certain co-worker, you may be entering into behavior that could potentially damage trust. If you find that you are seeking interactions with a certain individual for the purpose of stress relief, pleasure-seeking or novelty, it may be time to seek professional counsel in order to better understand your behavior.

What makes individuals look outside the marriage?

Following are some of the causal factors that may lead a spouse to be open to extramarital relationships:

- Lack of marital sexual satisfaction – While an emotional connection may remain in a marriage, a spouse may see the frustration of little or no sexual satisfaction as justification for looking elsewhere. If so, what may start as seemingly innocent conversation may easily lead to more intense experiences.

- Alternate sexual preferences – While understanding that there may be many reasons to enter into a traditional marriage, for some individuals, sexual orientation may include the desire to be with a same sex partner, more than one partner, or with someone participating in sexual practices not acceptable to one's spouse. Searching for alternate sexual satisfaction may become an increasingly powerful magnet for out-of-marriage liaisons.

- Insecurity about sexual desirability – Societal and familial messages go a long way toward determining our self-perceptions as sexual beings. At times, people do not feel that their spouses see them as sufficiently sexual. The result may be searching for sexual self-esteem and confirmation outside the marriage.

- Expressing rage/hurt – In these instances, there is less of a desire for sexual satisfaction, and more of an intention to cause emotional damage to one's partner. Whether revealed passively or openly, maintaining the secret is only a temporary stage, since the emotional pain can occur only if the extramarital connection becomes known.

- Acting out – Sometimes an affair occurs as an expression of an unhealthy or controlling dynamic between partners. One couple presented to one of our clinics after the wife discovered that the husband had engaged in an affair. After processing the betrayal, we explored the marital dynamics. In this marriage, the husband perceived his angry wife's control and disapproval of him as infantilizing. As he was essentially conflict-avoidant, they did not confront one another and communicate in a healthy way. Acting out sexually was a response to this marital dynamic in which he felt treated as a child, and he punished her with this affair.

- Mid-life crisis – This may be more mythical than real, but for some it can turn into a potent motivator. Aging does not come gracefully to everyone, and spouses may desire to relive an idealized stage when sex was supposedly more available with little commensurate responsibility. While this crisis may be transitional, it has the potential for planting the seeds of destruction.

- Search for vitality – Sometimes sexual connections outside of the marriage stem from a personal journey to fill a void or to experience vitality. This may happen despite a satisfying marriage, resulting from an individual rather than relational crisis. It could occur after the loss of a parent or loss of a job, and requires a deeper understanding of the meaning of the affair.

If you find that your marriage is challenged by any of these issues, we strongly encourage you to seek professional help. In addition, before couples discuss details with each other concerning any extramarital activity, it may be wise that each consults a rabbi individually, as important *halachic* considerations may affect the viability of the marriage, particularly for the woman engaged in the affair.

Healing from infidelity

Marital and sex therapist Esther Perel, author of *The State of Affairs: Rethinking Infidelity* divides affair recovery into three main steps – the crisis, the insight, and the vision. In the crisis phase, the couple is in the fight, flight or freeze mode, such that a therapy process should not only help a couple get past the crisis, but also help rebuild and reconnect once the couple is no longer reactive. We offer several guidelines to this process in the immediate aftermath of revealing the affair:

- Don't be hasty – Agree to avoid any immediate major decisions about the marriage.

- Reality check – Be sure your suspicions about your spouse are as accurate as possible and avoid assumptions.

- Avoid payback – It will resolve nothing.

- Don't involve the children – Try to minimize family damage and do not use the children as weapons.

- Keep your distance – Allow physical distance from one another as necessary.

In the crisis phase, emotions run high. The betrayed partner is often in a state of shock. He or she may feel alternately numb, angry, sad, frustrated and/or overwhelmed. He or she may ruminate and obsess about the details of the affair, though the initial phase may not be the best time to ask insight-oriented questions, such as, "What did the affair mean for you?" This occurs during the insight phase.

In some cases, the shock to the betrayed partner may result in such intense feelings that he or she is unable to engage reflectively in a couple process, and may require an initial phase of individual therapy. The partner who had the affair may also require individual sessions in the therapy process.

Moving on to the next phases requires emotional processing. The betrayed partner will need to feel understood, and the partner who had the affair will need to authentically express regret for the pain that was caused and to provide empathy and compassion.

Each spouse must speak honestly and truthfully, whether about the out-of-marriage contacts or the state of the marriage itself. Weigh your options, short term and long term, and try to clarify your goals.

The partner who had the affair also needs to process his or her feelings, including guilt, anger and resentment, and grief around the ending of the affair. He or she may also need to resolve the blame that he or she attaches to the partner for causing the affair by withholding intimacy. These feelings should be discussed with a therapist who can help the couple ask each other insight-oriented questions for greater understanding and healing, and help them move toward the final stage of recovery.

The final stages of the process involve healing the breach and the violation of trust, and looking critically at the relationship in order to rebuild what may have been lost. This requires examining how to strengthen the relationship to avoid future crises and to recreate a relationship that may even become stronger and more powerful in the aftermath of the affair.

While this is not easy, and while some couples do dissolve their marriage in the aftermath of an affair, from our experience, it is possible to reestablish trust and rebuild the relationship.

Parting Thoughts

Let your marriage always be "Kedat Moshe ve-Yisrael" – modeled after Matan Torah, and thus full of joy, love and the excitement of discovery and newness. Let your home become both a Mt. Sinai and a Ohel Moed (Tent of Meeting) for the ongoing and creative experience of Matan Torah within the dynamics of Jewish marriage.

A s marital therapists and sexual health professionals, we believe that your sex life can connect you to one another not only physically, but emotionally and even spiritually. We hope that the tools we have provided will help you create and experience an emotional and sexual connection that will allow you to wake up each morning smiling at each other with satisfaction and love.

We conclude with two Hasidic insights related to sexual enjoyment:

I once heard a modest man bemoan the fact that it is human nature to have physical pleasure from sex. He preferred that there be no feeling of pleasure at all, so that he could have sex solely to fulfill the command of his Creator... and I thought that way myself... Later, however, God favored me with a gift of grace, granting me understanding of the true meaning of sanctification during sexual intercourse: that it comes precisely from feeling physical pleasure. This secret is wondrous, deep and awesome.

Rabbi Baruch of Kosov, Amud Haavoda, p. 29b

Rabbi Tzvi Hirsh of Ziditchov taught his disciples "before sexual intercourse, they should give thanks to God, in their spoken language, for the pleasure that He created."

Rabbi Naphtali Hertz, Yifrach biYamav Tzaddik, p. 48b

We wish you marital health and happiness. May your intimate lives together be wondrous, deep and meaningful.

References and Further Readings

Emotional Intimacy

Hold Me Tight: Your Guide to the Most Successful Approach to Building Loving Relationship (2011) by Sue Johnson

Passionate Marriage: Keeping Love and Intimacy Alive in Committed Relationships (2009) by David Schnarch

Wired for Love: How Understanding Your Partner's Brain and Attachment Style Can Help You Diffuse Conflict and Build a Secure Relationship (2012) by Stan Taktin

The Five Love Languages: The Secret to Love That Lasts (2010) Gary Chapman

Men and Sex

Men's Sexual Health: Fitness for Satisfying Sex (2007) by Barry W. McCarthy and Michael E. Metz

The New Male Sexuality, Revised Edition (1999) by Bernie Zilbergeld

Women and Sex

Come as You Are: The Surprising New Science That Will Transform Your Sex Life (2015) by Emily Nagoski

Sex Matters for Women, Second Edition: A Complete Guide to Taking Care of Your Sexual Self (2011) by Sallie Foley, Sally A. Kope and Dennis P. Sugrue

The Elusive Orgasm: A Woman's Guide to Why She Can't and How she Can Orgasm (2008) by Vivienne Cass

For Yourself: The Fulfillment of Female Sexuality (2015) by Lonnie Barbach

Couples and Sex

Love Worth Making: How to Have Ridiculously Great Sex in a Long-Lasting Relationship (2018) by Stephen Snyder

Mating in Captivity: Unlocking Erotic Intelligence (2012) by Esther Perel

Rekindling Desire, Second Edition (2013) by Barry McCarthy and Emily McCarthy

The Joy of Sex: The Timeless Guide to Lovemaking, Ultimate Revised Edition (2009) by Alex Comfort and Susan Quilliam

Getting the Sex You Want (2008) by Tammy Nelson

Sex and Trauma

The Courage to Heal: A Guide for Women Survivors of Child Sexual Abuse (2015) by Ellen Bass and Laura Davis

The Sexual Healing Journey: A Guide for Survivors of Sexual Abuse, Third Edition (2012) by Wendy Maltz

The Survivors Guide to Sex: How to Have an Empowered Sex Life After Child Sexual Abuse (1999) by Staci Haines

Victims No Longer: The Classic Guide for Men Recovering from Sexual Child Abuse (2014) by Mike Lew

Sex and Aging

Naked at Our Age: Talking Out Loud About Senior Sex (2011) by Joan Price

Sex and Love at Midlife: It's Better than Ever (2010) by Bernie Zilbergeld and George Zilbergeld

Sex and Cancer

Prostate Cancer and the Man You Love: Supporting and Caring for Your Partner (2015) by Anne Katz

Women Cancer Sex (2009) by Anne Katz

Women and Sexual Pain

> *Healing Painful Sex: A Woman's Guide to Confronting, Diagnosing and Treating Sexual Pain (2011) by Deborah Coady and Nancy Fish*
>
> *The V Book: A Doctor's Guide to Complete Vulvovaginal Health (2008) by Elizabeth G. Stewart and Paula Spencer*
>
> *A Woman's Guide to Overcoming Sexual Fear and Pain (2015) by Aurelie Jones Goodwin and Marc E. Agronin*

Sex and Disability

> *The Facts of Life… and More: Sexuality and Intimacy for People with Intellectual Disabilities (2007) by Leslie Walker-Hirsch*
>
> *The Ultimate Guide to Sex and Disabilities: For All of Us Who Live with Disabilities, Chronic Pain, and Illness (2016) by Miriam Kaufman, Cory Silverberg and Fran Odette*

Sex and Sexuality in the Jewish Tradition

Books:

> *The Newlywed Guide to Physical Intimacy (2011) by David Ribner and Jennie Rosenfeld*
>
> *A Lifetime Companion to the Laws of Jewish Family Life, Third revised edition (2011) by Deena Zimmerman, Foreword by Rabbi Yehuda Henkin and Afterword by Talli Rosenbaum*
>
> *Halachik Positions: What Judaism Really Says about Passion in the Marital Bed (2015) by Yaakov Shapiro*

Additional Resources:

> *Intimate Judaism podcast with Talli Rosenbaum and Rabbi Scott Kahn* www.IntimateJudaism.com
>
> *The Eden Center* www.TheEdenCenter.com

Merkaz Yahel www.MerkazYahel.org.il/en

The Academy of Jewish Intimacy
http://AcademyofJewishIntimacy.com

Kosher Sensuality: David Ribner's Facebook page:
https://www.facebook.com/Kosher-Sensuality

Talli Rosenbaum's website www.TalliRosenbaum.com

Ve-ahavtem pleasure product store:
https://www.ve-ahavtem.com/english

Talli Yehuda Rosenbaum earned a Master's degree in Clinical Sociology and Counseling and a certificate in Mental Health Studies from the University of North Texas at Neve Yerushalayim. She is an individual and couple therapist and is certified as a sex therapist by The American Association of Sexuality Educators, Counselors and Therapists (AASECT), as well as the Israeli Society for Sex Therapy (ISST). The author of over 40 peer reviewed journal articles and book chapters on sexual health, sexual pain disorders, unconsummated marriage, and sexuality and Judaism, she is the co-editor of the Springer textbook entitled *The Overactive Pelvic Floor* and an associate editor of *Sexual Medicine Reviews*. In addition to maintaining an active private practice, Talli is the academic advisor for Yahel: The Center for Jewish Intimacy. Talli lectures frequently in Israel and abroad, to both professional and lay audiences. Together with Rabbi Scott Kahn, she co-hosts a monthly podcast called "Intimate Judaism."

David S. Ribner earned his BA, Rabbinic Ordination, MS and MSW degrees from Yeshiva University and his doctorate from Columbia University. He is the founder and chairman of the Sex Therapy Training Program, Bar-Ilan University, Israel and is certified as a sex therapist and supervisor in the U.S and Israel. He is in private practice as a sex and marital therapist in Jerusalem, has authored some 40 articles and book chapters and writes and lectures extensively on cultural sensitivity and sexuality. He is also the co-author (along with Jennie Rosenfeld) of *Et Le'ehov (A Time to Love): The Newlywed's Guide to Physical Intimacy*, helping understand the interface between tradition and sexuality. He is an Associate Editor of the journal *Sexual and Relationship Therapy*, and in addition to the American Association of Sexuality Educators, Counselors and Therapists (AASECT), is a member of the Israel Society for Sex Therapy and the International Academy for Sex Research.